PRÉPARER ET RÉUSSIR LE TOEFL iBT®

Éditions d'Organisation
Groupe Eyrolles
61, bd Saint-Germain
75240 Paris Cedex 05
www.editions-organisation.com
www.editions-eyrolles.com

L'ANGLAIS
CHEZ LE MÊME ÉDITEUR

- *Préparer et réussir le TOEIC*
  S. Marko-Michel et C. Caillat
- *Préparer et réussir le GMAT*
  S. Marko-Michel et C. Caillat
- *Intervenir dans une réunion en anglais comme en français,*
  Édition bilingue, Bénédicte Lapeyre
- *Transport-logistique, lexique français-anglais/anglais-français,*
  P.-J.-B. Bouyer et B. Mc Cormick
- *Téléphoner en anglais – Phoning in english,*
  P. Levanti et J. Studer-Laurens
- *Correspondance commerciale français-anglais,*
  V. Schoenwald

ISBN : 978-2-7081-3633-5

Sommaire

Introduction

Druide : Prends un peu de potion magique, on ne sait jamais !
Astérix : Est-ce bien nécessaire ? Nous n'irons pas loin et il n'y a personne de ce côté.

Une aventure d'Astérix le Gaulois, *La grande traversée*

Vous allez passer le TOEFL iBT… une université ou une école vous l'a demandé. Alors, comment comptez-vous préparer cet examen ? Vous allez faire comme d'habitude, non ? Réviser les verbes irréguliers, revoir la concordance des temps, réapprendre du vocabulaire… Cela marche avant tous les contrôles d'anglais, n'est-ce pas ? Vous trouvant vers la fin de votre scolarité, il se peut que vous vous posiez la même question qu'Astérix a posée au druide avant sa grande traversée : est-ce bien nécessaire ?

Oui mais voilà, les vieilles méthodes ne suffisent plus. Finis les jours où les universités et les écoles se satisfaisaient de candidats ayant une connaissance passive de l'anglais. Désormais, elles recherchent des étudiants déjà opérationnels dans la langue, capables d'intégrer un programme académique anglophone dès le premier jour. C'est pourquoi le TOEFL n'existe plus dans son ancien format, après quarante ans d'examens traditionnels.

Aujourd'hui, vous préparez le TOEFL iBT, dit « Next Generation ». Vous vous préparez à passer l'examen devant un écran d'ordinateur pendant quatre heures et demie et à parler anglais dans un micro. Vous vous préparez à accomplir successivement plusieurs actions :

- écouter une conférence et en parler
- lire un article, puis écouter une conférence et écrire un compte rendu à propos des deux à la fois.

Bref, vous vous préparez à une évaluation de votre capacité à manier l'anglais réel et non pas pédagogique. Le TOEFL iBT est un moyen pour votre université ou école de savoir comment vous communiquez dans le monde anglophone de nos jours. Cette capacité est un critère de décision pour votre candidature.

Grâce à la technologie de l'Internet, le TOEFL iBT, (Internet Based Test) établit un précédent dans le domaine linguistique. Désormais, l'évaluation de l'expression orale d'un candidat en anglais peut se faire de manière objective, efficace, et systématique. Finis aussi les jours de l'épreuve orale subjective, où l'avis de l'examinateur est maître de votre destin. Désormais, votre prestation orale passera par un système de notation standardisé.

Une question s'impose : comment vous situez-vous dans ce contexte ? Votre anglais est-t-il au point ? Pouvez-vous parcourir rapidement les longs textes qui sont soumis à votre lecture du TOEFL iBT ? Où en sont vos aptitudes rédactionnelles ? Pouvez-vous rédiger plus de 300 mots en 30 minutes directement sur un clavier QWERTY ? Saurez-vous écouter et comprendre les maîtres de conférence américains lors de leurs longues interventions à l'examen ? Saurez-vous prendre des notes efficaces ? Et votre expression orale, comment se compare-t-elle à celle d'autres candidats qui parlent anglais depuis leur enfance ?

Comment allez-vous préparer le TOEFL iBT ? A vous de réagir. Allez-vous vous contenter de vos méthodes habituelles et compter sur votre bagage d'anglais scolaire ? Ou chercherez-vous un coup de pouce supplémentaire pour mieux vous préparer face à ce nouveau défi ?

Et si vous commenciez votre préparation tout de suite en prenant le CD-ROM de ce livre, pour passer le diagnostic test dans les mêmes conditions que le jour où vous passerez le TOEFL iBT. Ce test a été conçu pour vous aiguiller vers vos points faibles en anglais. Il vous permettra aussi de comprendre immédiatement comment se présente le TOEFL iBT et ses techniques d'évaluation, explications à l'appui.

Les chapitres qui suivent le diagnostic test vous mettront sur la bonne voie, en vous donnant des conseils concrets et en vous livrant des astuces pour le jour J. Ils vous fourniront des méthodes pour mieux gérer la masse de textes que vous aurez à traiter en temps limité.

Pendant quarante ans, le TOEFL a été un examen de questions à choix multiple, scientifiquement construites pour que les candidats commettent des erreurs. Aujourd'hui, plus que jamais, le TOEFL iBT est un examen qui doit obligatoirement se préparer.

Première partie

INFORMEZ-VOUS

CHAPITRE 1

Que devez-vous savoir sur le TOEFL iBT avant de commencer à le préparer ?

1. Qu'est-ce que le TOEFL iBT ?
2. Pourquoi ce TOEFL nouvelle génération ?
3. Quelles sont les aptitudes évaluées par le TOEFL iBT ?

1. Qu'est-ce que le TOEFL iBT ?

Le TOEFL iBT (Test of English as a Foreign Language – Internet Based Test) est la nouvelle version du TOEFL, dit « Next Generation ». Il remplace le TOEFL sur papier et le TOEFL CBT (Computer Based Test). Le TOEFL iBT (Internet-Based Test) est administré sur internet dans des centres sécurisés depuis la fin du mois d'octobre 2005.

L' iBT fournit le moyen d'enregistrer la partie orale du test et de l'envoyer par internet à l'ETS pour notation. L'étudiant qui passe le TOEFL iBT parle dans son micro durant la partie *Speaking*, ses réponses sont enregistrées digitalement et envoyées à « ETS Online Scoring Network ».

A la différence du TOEFL CBT, le TOEFL iBT n'est pas « *computer-adaptive* », c'est-à-dire qu'il ne s'adaptera pas à votre niveau d'anglais. Chaque candidat aura des questions de même difficulté.

Le TOEFL iBT est le seul examen standardisé qui comprend des « Integrated tasks » (tâches intégrées). Ces tâches font appel à quatre aptitudes : l'écoute, la lecture, l'expression orale, et l'écriture. C'est un reflet très réaliste de l'utilisation de la langue dans la vie courante. Cela permet d'évaluer votre aptitude de communiquer dans le milieu universitaire.

Le contenu de l'examen est tiré d'une base de données de l'anglais écrit et parlé. Cette base de données contient plus de 2.7 millions de mots, utilisés dans les universités américaines. En ce qui concerne le langage parlé, les mots de la base de données sont ceux qui sont utilisés lors des conférences, travaux pratiques, groupes de travail et des interactions en facultés.

Tout cela pour vous montrer que l'anglais du TOEFL iBT, c'est vraiment l'anglais entendu et parlé sur les campus américains !

2. Pourquoi ce TOEFL nouvelle génération ?

Le but du TOEFL a toujours été d'évaluer les compétences en anglais des non anglophones.

Il est surtout utilisé par les universités aux Etats-Unis dans leurs procédures d'admission des étudiants étrangers, mais aussi par des entreprises dans leurs procédures de recrutement de non anglophones.

Le TOEFL iBT a été conçu pour être un meilleur indicateur que les versions précédentes du TOEFL de l'aptitude d'un étudiant d'utiliser l'anglais dans le milieu universitaire. Le niveau d'anglais de l'examen est plus proche du niveau utilisé dans une université américaine et il évalue en profondeur l'aptitude à communiquer à l'oral et à l'écrit. Ceci est très important, car pour réussir des études et s'intégrer à l'université, il faut pouvoir s'exprimer avec aisance à l'oral comme à l'écrit. Il ne suffit pas de bien lire et comprendre.

Ces exigences au niveau du TOEFL iBT présentent aussi des avantages pour les étudiants. Car un étudiant qui a le projet de suivre ses études dans une université américaine a besoin de savoir avec quel niveau d'anglais il doit arriver aux USA. Même avant d'envisager de s'inscrire au TOEFL iBT, il peut, en étudiant ce que l'on demande à cet examen, se faire une idée très précise du niveau d'anglais qu'il lui faut atteindre et de ses lacunes.

Un programme de travail destiné à préparer le TOEFL iBT est aussi un excellent moyen d'atteindre le niveau d'anglais qui permettra de réussir ses études aux USA. La préparation du TOEFL iBT ne doit pas être entreprise seulement comme une préparation à l'examen, mais aussi comme une préparation à l'enseignement et à la vie universitaire américaine.

Voici les principales nouveautés dans le TOEFL iBT :

- Le TOEFL iBT teste 4 compétences : compréhension écrite/orale, expression écrite/orale
- Une partie « Speaking » qui comprend 6 tâches et est enregistrée
- Lancé depuis novembre 2005 en France, le TOEFL iBT est administré via internet dans les centres de tests habilités (CTAS).
- Integrated Tasks – des questions qui font appel à plusieurs compétences à la fois ; par exemple lire, écouter et puis parler – dans le but de reproduire l'utilisation de la langue dans les situations de la vie réelle
- La prise des notes est permise dans toutes les parties de l'examen
- La grammaire est intégrée dans chaque partie ; il n'y a plus de partie « Grammar »
- Les conférences et conversations à écouter sont plus longues ; jusqu'à cinq minutes

- La langue dans les conférences et conversations correspond à la langue qu'on entend tous les jours. Il y a des hésitations, des pauses, des digressions, etc.
- Les instructions sont données au début de chaque partie de l'examen.

L'examen comprend 4 parties et dure environ 4 heures.

PARTIE	FORMAT	QUESTIONS	TEMPS ALLOUE
Reading	3 à 5 textes d'environ 700 mots	12 à 14 par texte	60 à 100 minutes
Listening	4 à 6 conférences de 3 à 5 minutes 2 à 3 conversations de 3 à 5 minutes	6 questions par conférence 5 questions par conversation	60 à 90 minutes
Pause			10 minutes
Speaking	2 Independent Speaking 4 Integrated Speaking	Pour chaque tâche il y a 15 secondes de préparation et ensuite l'enregistrement qui dure de 45 à 60 secondes	20 minutes (temps d'écoute et de lecture compris)
Writing	1 Integrated Writing 1 Independent Writing		20 minutes 30 minutes
		Temps au total	4 heures (approximatif)

Sur le site officiel du TOEFL iBT (www.ets.org) il y a un « message board » où des personnes ayant déjà passé le TOEFL iBT parlent de leur expérience de l'examen. Il y a aussi un échange d'idées sur l'examen et la façon de le préparer.

3. Quelles sont les aptitudes évaluées par le TOEFL iBT ?

Reading : Cette partie mesure votre aptitude à comprendre des textes du style « college textbook » (manuel d'université). Les textes sont longs – environ 700 mots, et assez difficiles. Les questions varient. Il y a des questions style QCM classique, qui portent sur la compréhension et les détails, et aussi des questions qui vous demandent de remplir des tableaux, d'ajouter des phrases dans la partie appropriée du texte, ou autre.

Listening : Cette partie mesure votre aptitude à comprendre l'anglais nord-américain. C'est l'anglais du milieu universitaire, avec son vocabulaire et ses expressions spécifiques. Les textes sont des extraits des conférences, des conversations entre étudiants et professeurs ou avec d'autres personnes du milieu universitaire. Les questions varient. Il y a des QCMs classiques, qui portent sur la compréhension et les détails. Il y a aussi des questions qui demandent de mettre des éléments en ordre, de les associer, les relier, ou de remplir un tableau.

Speaking : Cette partie mesure votre aptitude à vous exprimer en anglais. Les tâches « Independent Speaking » vous demandent d'exposer votre opinion ou votre expérience. Les tâches « Integrated Speaking » vous demandent d'écouter/lire un texte et de l'expliquer ou le commenter. Vous avez 15 secondes pour le préparer et le temps d'enregistrement est de 45 à 60 secondes.

Writing : Cette partie mesure votre aptitude à écrire un texte en anglais, en utilisant un ordinateur équipé d'un clavier QWERTY. La partie « Independent Writing » vous demande de présenter votre opinion ou votre expérience. La partie « Integrated Writing » vous demande de lire/écouter un texte et d'écrire sur ce sujet.

CHAPITRE 2

Les renseignements pratiques

1. Le déroulement du TOEFL iBT, de l'inscription aux résultats
2. Les outils d'aide à la préparation

Le TOEFL iBT est conçu et géré par Educational Testing Service®, organisation à but non lucratif se trouvant à Princeton, New Jersey (US), spécialisée dans l'évaluation depuis 1947. Elle compte 2600 spécialistes, elle est présente dans 180 pays et administre chaque année dans le monde plus de 24 millions de tests académiques et professionnels.

1. Le déroulement du TOEFL iBT, de l'inscription aux résultats

LES INSCRIPTIONS

Quand s'inscrire ?

On peut s'inscrire au TOEFL iBT toute l'année sur rendez-vous. Dernier délai d'inscription par internet ou par téléphone : 7 jours ouvrables à l'avance. Dernier délai par courrier : un mois avant la date d'examen.

Où et comment ?

Par internet (fortement recommandé) : taper l'adresse www.ets.org/toefl, ensuite Learners and Test Takers. Ouvrez un compte utilisateur. Confirmation immédiate de la réservation. Suivez les consignes ; 24 heures sur 24.

Par téléphone : appeler Thomson Prometric au Pays-Bas au 31-320-239-540 (e-mail : euregs@thomson.com) pendant les heures du bureau. Vous recevrez un numéro de confirmation et l'adresse exacte de votre centre d'examen.

Par courrier : obtenir le formulaire d'inscription par internet ou en contactant un représentant en France (01 40 75 95 20 à Paris, e-mail contact-fr@etseurope.org ou 04.72.07.46.64 à Lyon, e-mail toeiclyon@etseurope.org). Le formulaire se trouve dans la publication intitulée Information and Registration Bulletin. Cette publication peut être commandée sur Internet sur www.ets.org/toefl, sinon téléchargée à la même adresse. Envoyez le formulaire rempli à :

Thomson Prometric
ATTN : PTC Registrations Europe
P. O. Box 2024
8203 AA Lelystad PAYS-BAS

Combien cela coûte ?

- $140 l'inscription
- $40 le changement de date
- $20 la revalidation de résultats que vous avez annulés
- $17 la communication des résultats à une école au-delà de la limite de quatre communications gratuites
- $20 le chèque à découvert

Avec quels modes de paiement ?

- Carte de crédit (seuls modes de paiement par internet et par téléphone)
- E-check
- Mandat
- Chèque en dollars
- Chèque en euros émis d'une banque de la zone euro (Attention : utiliser le taux de change TTS, Telegraphic Transfer Selling)

Les remboursements sont-ils possibles ?

- $65, si vous annulez trois jours avant la date prévue (sinon, pas de remboursement)

Quelles prestations pour les candidats handicapés ?

- Des prestations spécifiques sont disponibles pour les candidats invalides. Contactez par e-mail : stassd@ets.org pour plus de renseignements ou appelez le 31-320-239-540.

Le jour de l'examen

L'arrivée

Il est demandé aux candidats d'arriver une demi-heure à l'avance. Il faut donc compter une présence de quatre heures et demie en tout.

La carte d'identité et les pièces d'identité

Attention, si un problème se pose au moment de la vérification de votre identité, l'entrée à la salle d'examen vous sera refusée et vous n'aurez le droit à aucun remboursement. Il faut donc de la rigueur à ce sujet et vous munir de votre carte d'identité.

Il faut une pièce d'identité avec une photo récente et une signature. Les noms et prénoms doivent correspondre à l'inscription (pas de diminutifs). Les pièces acceptées sont : carte d'identité nationale (CIN), passeport, permis de conduire, carte militaire. La signature sera vérifiée.

Si, par erreur, il manque une signature ou une photo sur la première pièce, alors il faut présenter une deuxième pièce : carte d'étudiant, lettre manuscrite de votre école.

Liste des pièces non-acceptées : CIN périmée, carte de crédit, carte de sécurité sociale, carte de la conduite accompagnée, permis de conduire international, carte d'étudiant internationale, carte de travail, lettre manuscrite ou document signés par l'huissier.

Les affaires

Chaque candidat est tenu de déposer ses affaires (y compris le téléphone portable) dans une consigne sur place où l'on décline toute responsabilité de vol. L'accès aux affaires personnelles est interdit pendant la durée de l'examen. Si vous utilisez votre téléphone portable pendant la pause, vous serez exclu de l'examen sans remboursement.

Attestation et photo

Chaque candidat doit s'engager à garder l'examen confidentiel par la signature d'une attestation et doit se faire photographier devant son ordinateur. Cette photo sera jointe au résultat du TOEFL iBT. La signature de l'attestation et la photo sont toutes les deux obligatoires.

Levez le doigt

Vous devez lever le doigt si vous avez besoin de quitter la salle (la pendule ne s'arrêtant pas) ou si vous avez un problème informatique.

Annulation de résultat, renvoi du centre d'examen

On peut renvoyer un candidat : s'il passe l'examen pour quelqu'un d'autre ou si quelqu'un le passe pour lui, s'il dépasse la pause de dix minutes, si sa pièce d'identité n'est pas valable, s'il a obtenu des questions de l'examen à l'avance, s'il utilise un téléphone portable, s'il utilise des aides (calculatrice, dictionnaire, pendule, etc.), s'il dérange les autres candidats, s'il essaie d'emporter son brouillon, s'il trafique l'ordinateur, ou s'il apporte de la nourriture, des boissons, du tabac au centre. L'ETS se réserve le droit d'interdire à un candidat de passer le TOEFL iBT non seulement le jour de l'examen, mais aussi à l'avenir.

Le résultat

Le résultat est communiqué par internet quinze jours ouvrables après la date de l'examen (accès avec votre numéro d'inscription). Ensuite, il est posté et communiqué aux écoles que vous avez indiquées.

A la fin de chaque session, le candidat peut annuler son examen. Dans ce cas, c'est comme si l'examen n'avait jamais existé : le résultat n'est communiqué à personne, même pas au candidat.

Renseignements supplémentaires
Pour tout renseignement supplémentaire, consultez www.toefl.org, le site officiel de l'ETS. Il est pratique et complet.

2. Les outils d'aide à la préparation

Si vous avez accès à l'Internet des outils de préparation sont à votre portée pour mieux préparer le TOEFL iBT. Voici une liste de nos « petits sites préférés », en commençant par l'aspect linguistique :

http://www.eslcafe.com
http://www.englishclub.com
http://a4esl.org/
http://www.tesol.net/teslact.html
http :/www.esl-lab.com
http :/www.manythings.org
http://www.esldesk.com/esl-links
http://members.aol.com/eslkathy/esl.htm
http://www.ohiou.edu/esl/english
http://iteslj.org/ESL.html

Nous vous recommandons également des sites aidant tout étudiant à développer ses compétences pour passer des examens rédigés en anglais :

www.ucc.vt.edu/stdyhlp.html
www.asu.edu/duas/wcenter
www.yorku.ca/cdc/lsp
www.sas.calpoly.edu/asc
www.wisc.edu/writing/Handbook/Documentation.html
http://owl.english.purdue.edu/index.html

Pour améliorer la lecture de textes académiques et littéraires, nous recommandons :

www.wikipedia.com
http://www.gutenberg.org
www.ipl.org

et pour la lecture de journaux, essayez :

http://www.onlinenewspapers.com/usstate/usatable.htm
http://www.latimes.com
http://sfgate.com/chronicle
http://www.boston.com/globe
http://www.iht.com
http://www.nytimes.com
http://www.usatoday.com

ou cherchez le quotidien de votre choix avec un moteur de recherche.

Enfin, pour l'entraînement à la compréhension auditive, consultez :

http://www.elllo.org/et ses liens intéressants
http://www.breakingnewsenglish.com/

Deuxième partie

TESTEZ VOTRE NIVEAU DE DÉPART

CHAPITRE 3

Évaluez votre niveau de départ avec le Diagnostic Test

1. Reading Section
2. Listening Section
3. Speaking Section
4. Writing Section

Voici la transcription du Diagnostic Test qui se trouve sur le CD-rom joint à ce livre. Passez l'examen sur ordinateur en utilisant le CD-rom. Après cela, ce chapitre vous servira à faire une étude plus approfondie du Diagnostic Test.

1. Reading section

Directions

You have 60 minutes to read all of the passages and answer the questions. Some passages include a word or phrase that is underlined in blue. Click on the word or phrase to see a definition or an explanation.

To move on to the next question, click **Next**. You can skip questions and go back to them later as long as time remains. To return to previous questions, click **Back**. You may click **Review** at any time and the review screen shows you which questions you have answered and which you have not. From the Review screen, you may go directly to any question you have already seen in the Reading section.

When you are ready to continue, click on the **Dismiss Directions** icon.

Reading 1

Speleology is the scientific study of caves and other karst features: their make-up, biology, historical aspects, physical characteristics, formation and development are all studied in detail by researchers. Lava tubes and blisters are the two types of primary caves whose formation takes place at the same time as the rock surrounding them. However, sea, ice, solutional, fracture, and talus caves are all dug into the rock after the surrounding rock itself has undergone removal processes, such as solution or erosion. [] The most prevalent of these secondary caves is the solutional type, composed of rock which is soluble, such as limestone, dolomite, salt, sandstone, and gypsum. [] For instance, it is commonplace for rainwater or groundwater to wear down limestone as a result of its movement and its chemical composition, most especially its carbonic acid

(CO2). [] This dissolution produces an easily-defineable landform known as karst, characterized by sinkholes and underground drainage. []

Limestone caves are often lavished with calcium carbonate formations, which look like enormous canine teeth sprouting from the ceiling and the floor (stalactites and stalagmites). These secondary mineral deposits in caves are known as speleothems, as observed in the Lechuguilla Cave. This is the deepest limestone cave in the United States (489 meters), located in Carlsbad Caverns National Park, within its 46,768-acre area in the southeastern corner of New Mexico. Helictites are also observed in the Caverns, these being unusual formations which grow in every direction, paying no particular attention to the laws of gravity. Such helictites and other rare formations are composed of calcite and aragonite.

Animal cave dwellers are categorized as troglobites (cave-limited species), troglophiles (species which can live their entire lives in caves, but can also be found in other environments), trogloxenes (species which use caves, but are required to leave these caves to complete their life cycle) and accidentals. Of these animals, the troglobites are among the most peculiar of beings, often with features such as a loss of eyes, loss of pigment, longer appendages, and a development of keener additional senses to the five senses we know as humans (for example, an ability to sense vibrations in water).

Approximately one million Mexican Free-tailed Bats live in the Carlsbad Caverns, crowding together on the ceiling of Bat Cave, a passageway near the natural entrance, during the sunlit hours of the day. This daytime refuge is the destination of migrating bats from Mexico who give birth to their young in June of each year. At dusk, a swarm of thousands of these flying mammals exits the cave in a whirlwind to feed in the Pecos and Black River valleys where each bat eats several stomachfuls of moths and other insects before dawn.

Throughout ages in time, primitive peoples and tribes have used caves for shelter, burial, or as religious sites. Aside from their geological and biological aspects, this makes caves an archaeological treasure house for learning about these many peoples.

Glossary:

- to sprout from: to grow from
- a swarm: a large group

1. The word prevalent in the passage is closest in meaning to
   - A. important
   - B. predominant
   - C. deep
   - D. worthy

2. The word its in the passage refers to
   - A. limestone
   - B. carbonic acid
   - C. rainwater
   - D. commonplace

3. According to paragraph 1, what is a good example of a primary cave?
   - A. A limestone cave worn down by groundwater.
   - B. An ice cave in a glacier.
   - C. An eroded lava solutional cave.
   - D. A tube formation in lava during eruption.

4. The word lavished in the passage is closest in meaning to
   - A. adorned
   - B. covered
   - C. overflowing
   - D. pristine

5. Why does the author mention speleothems?
   - A. To describe interior formations in karst landforms.
   - B. To explain the geological aspects of primary caves.
   - C. To argue that solutional caves are often made of limestone.
   - D. To give details about historical aspects of mineral deposits.

6. The word dwellers in the passage is closest in meaning to
   - A. citizens
   - B. survivors
   - C. creatures
   - D. inhabitants

7. According to the the categories stated in the text, how can a Mexican Free-tailed Bat be defined?
   - A. As a trogloxene
   - B. As an accidental
   - C. As a troglobite
   - D. As a troglophile

8. How could a Mexican Free-tailed Bat's diet be described?
   - A. Well-balanced
   - B. Meager
   - C. Vegetarian
   - D. Hearty

9. The word peculiar in the passage is closest in meaning to
   - A. strange
   - B. handicapped
   - C. stunning
   - D. gorgeous

10. According to paragraph 5, tribes used caves
    A. to store their hunted meat and animal fur.
    B. to bless their meals.
    C. to shelter their hunting tools.
    D. to lay their dead in the tomb.

11. All of the following are cited as characteristics of the Mexican Free-tailed Bat EXCEPT
    A. This mammal has several abodes.
    B. The Mexican Free-tailed Bat migrates more than twenty miles.
    C. The bat is mobilized after the sun has set.
    D. The bat is a member of a solitary species.

12. Four squares ([]) indicate where the following sentence can be added to the passage.

    As a matter of fact, limestone solution is the origin of the majority of all caves on Earth.

    Where would the sentence best fit into the passage?

13. An introductory sentence for a brief summary of the passage is provided below. Complete the summary by choosing THREE answer choices that express the most important ideas in the passage. Some sentences do not belong in the summary because they express ideas that are not presented in the passage or are minor ideas in the passage. **This question is worth 2 points.**

    Caves are fascinating scientific phenomena which have been studied by researchers for many reasons.

    *
    *
    *

In fact, speleologists have determined the two contrasting formations of both primary and secondary caves.

As a matter of fact, talus and ice caves are still being perused by scientists today.

Solutional caves dug into limestone often contain stalactites and can lodge animals.

One million Mexican Free-tailed Bats live in the Carlsbad Caverns in New Mexico.

Not only do animals live in caves: human beings lived there long ago, seeking shelter and leaving their archaeological treasures.

In conclusion, primitive tribes lived in caves for shelter and religious reasons.

Reading 2

The lack of universal health care in the United States is historically due to this country's firm belief in a political philosophy known as individualism. Contrary to Britain's Welfare State period from 1945 until the 1970's, during which the National Health Service was founded, promising to care for the British « from the cradle to the grave », the United States has always left health care in the domaine of individual responsibility. Europeans widely scoff at this behavior, feeling that their government or tax-funded health cares protect citizens from doctor's bills with « societal insurance ». Americans call such systems « socialized » or « national » medicine, infringing upon the individual's rights.

Individualism is the belief that individual liberty and self-reliance are the most important values in life. It implies a conflict with any authority or state which tries to thwart individual independence. If this political philosophy needed to be summed up in a few words, it could be defined as the principle of « MYOB » (Minding your own business). Historically, the United States was founded by citizens who had left their countries for religious or political reasons. Later influenced by the French revolution, these original Americans made « life, liberty, and the pursuit of happiness » their dearest ideals, as stated in the Declaration of Independence.

It is tempting to confuse individualism with ethical egoism, just like certain Japanese who interpret individualism as betrayal to group values, like family or firm. **Ethical egoism is the pursuit of one's self-interest with no regard for the well-being of other people.** According to this principle, whether an individual decides to take other people into consideration or not, his main objective is his self-interest. By definition, egoists only act to their advantage, whereas individualists want to liberate every single person from collective control. Brought back to the health care situation, individual responsibility in the United States means protection from government control, not a lack of well-being for fellow citizens. However, critics of individualism would argue that excessive individualism can impair individuals themselves.

Collectivism is the opposite of individualism. [] This political philosophy emphasizes the importance of the group as the basic unit of survival. [] The Israeli kibbutzim operates as a collectivist society, in which people live and farm together voluntarily without private ownership. [] An individual living in a collectivist culture has an « us » or « we » identity, as in Chinese Confucianism, in which being a « community man » with a « social personality » is valued. In economics, the concept of the commons prevails in which all valued commodities, such as national defense, information goods, and environmental goods, are believed to belong to the group and not to be privatized. [] The means of production and the resulting products are owned and used by the state.

Capitalism is an economic system in which most of the means of production are privately owned and operated. The etymology of the word « capitalism » has its roots in the ownership of animals. Its Latin root is « capitalis », from « kaput », meaning « head » of cattle. Certain currencies reflect this origin in animal ownership, for instance, buck (a deerskin), stock (livestock), peso (pecu), rupee (rupya). The first use of the word « capitalism » in English was by the novelist Thackeray in 1854 by which he meant having ownership of capital.

A question which then needs to be addressed concerns the basis of capitalism. Is capitalism truly based upon individuals, or is it based on the firms and institutions which define individuals' roles? Since participation in these institutions is an individual choice, capitalism can still be considered as individualistic. However, capitalism can also thrive in certain collectivism societies with individual choice. The only difference is what the choice is based on : individual need versus collective need.

14. The word scoff in the passage is closest in meaning to
    - A. oppose
    - B. deny
    - C. disdain
    - D. chuckle

15. According to this passage, why is there no universal health care in the United States ?
    - A. Because Americans believe in the pursuit of one's self-interest.
    - B. Because tax-funded healthcare is too expensive.

C. In order to protect citizens from government control.
D. In order to promote collectivism in the country.

16. The word it in the passage refers to
A. individualism
B. life
C. belief
D. self-reliance

17. The word thwart in the passage is closest in meaning to
A. cross
B. depict
C. warn
D. avoid

18. Why does the author refer to « ethical egoism » in this passage ?
A. Because they look out for their self-interest.
B. To prove that ethical egoists can take others into consideration.
C. Because it is easy to confuse individualists with ethical egoists.
D. To demonstrate the principle of « MYOB ».

19. Which of the sentences below best expresses the information in the highlighted statement in the passage ? The other choices change the meaning or leave out important information.
A. Ethical egoism is the satisfaction of one's needs, while thinking of the health of others.
B. Ethical egoism is a thought for oneself without even sending one's regards to others.
C. Ethical egoism is a person's interest in the well-being of others.
D. Ethical egoism is a quest for one's good alone.

20. The word impair in the passage is closest in meaning to
A. protect
B. kill
C. harm
D. affect

21. According to paragraph 4, which would be a good example of collectivism ?
A. A community whose laws abolish private property.
B. A town in which each farmer raises his own tomatoes.
C. A citizen who has a reputation of betrayal to his community.
D. A community which allots land to new members upon arrival.

22. Four squares ([]) indicate where the following sentence can be added to the passage.

Another example is the communist states which often collectivized most economic sectors, agriculture in particular.
Where would the sentence best fit into the passage?

23. In which of the following chapters would this passage most probably appear?
    A. Collectivism and the Israeli kibbutzim.
    B. Health care and capitalism.
    C. Individualism and its principles.
    D. Capitalism and its basis.

24. What does the author explain about the basis of capitalism?
    A. The word is derived from ownership of animals.
    B. Thackeray used the word to refer to ownership of capital.
    C. Capitalism can be considered as individualistic.
    D. It can be based both on individuals or on firms and institutions.

25. All of the following are mentioned in the passage to explain the American attitude towards lack of universal health care EXCEPT
    A. a deeply-imbedded belief in collective health care insurance.
    B. a firm belief in individualism and the protection of individuals from collective control.
    C. a contrast with ethical egoism because self-interest is not the only factor.
    D. emphasis on individual responsibility rather than that of the group.

26. An introductory sentence for a brief summary of the passage is provided below. Complete the summary by selecting the THREE answer choices that express the most important ideas in the passage. Some sentences do not belong in the summary because they express ideas that are not presented in the passage or are minor ideas in the passage. **This question is worth 2 points.**

Individualism is the belief that personal liberty is the most important value in life.

*
*
*

Britain's National Health Service promises to take care of citizens « from the cradle to the grave ».

A collectivist, in contrast with an individualist, has a « we » identity as in Chinese Confucianism.

The « MYOB » (Minding your own business) philosophy summarizes the principle of individualism, as revered by most Americans.

D The « MYOB » (Minding your own business) philosophy is not to be confused with ethical egoism which stops only at the pursuit of one's self-interest.

A « buck » (deerskin) finds its origins in the ownership of animals, as does « capitalism ».

F Is capitalism an expression of individualism (responding to individual needs) or of collectivism (responding to an institution's needs) ?

Reading 3

The coca plant is traditionally grown in the eastern Andes Mountains, in lower altitudes. For many generations, the coca plant has been used by Indians in Peru, Bolivia, and northern Argentina. The earliest coca leaves were discovered on the northern coast of Peru c. 2500-1800 B.C. These leaves are also sometimes eaten by a beige Colombian moth known as the Eloria noyesi. Coca seeds are planted on small pieces of land, called almacigas, in the shade. When these young plants have reached 40-60 centimeters in height, they are then transplanted into holes called aspi. Although the coca plant itself thrives in hot and humid surroundings, it is transplanted into a drier setting for more satisfactory leaf production. The final result is a plant reaching 2-3 meters in height with small clustered flowers which turn into red berries. The leaves are harvested in March, although there is an off-season crop in the fall. They are then dried in the sun and packed in bags.

During both the pre-Inca period and the Inca Empire, the coca plant was an intricate part of religious ceremonies. It was used for offerings to a number of pantheistic gods (earth, corn, etc.), and most especially to Inti, the Sun god. The coca plant was also used for its smoke during sacrifices during worship which sometimes lasted from sunrise to sunset. Coca leaves were also chewed by priests to communicate with various gods, « chacchar » being its Quechuan translation.

Indians have been chewing coca leaves for centuries, carrying pouches called « huallqui » containing a one day's supply with them. They were so commonplace in their daily lives that they became a part of everyday vocabulary. A « cocada » is a measure of distance corresponding to the amount of leaves chewed while walking from one point to another. It can also refer to a measurement in time, and more specifically the numbers of minutes it takes for the leaves to lose their flavor.

The coca plant is most commonly associated with cocaine, and it is a proven fact that coca chewers experience a numbing sensation in their mouths. [] Bearing this fact in mind, it probably comes as no surprise that the Incas performed skull surgery, using coca leaves to dull the pain of the surgery. [] The leaf, however, also contains protein and vitamins, and has had a history of providing strength to people in a region of the globe where both food and oxygen are limited in quantity. [] Research performed at Erasmus University has shown that the Incas were not addicted to coca leaves, which were used essentially for their nutrients. []

Aside from its obvious link with cocaine, the coca plant is also associated with the soft drink Coke. The Coca-Cola Company, located in Atlanta, Georgia, buys 115 tons of coca leaves from Peru and 105 tons from Bolivia each year to manufacture its beverage following a secret recipe. In 1855, John S. Pemberton named his invention « Coca-Cola » because it contained coca leaves, a stimulant (5 ounces per gallon), and kola nuts, a source of caffeine. These same ingredients are used to this day, except that the coca leaves used are leftovers after cocaine-extraction, completely devoid of stimulant.

Cocaine stimulates the central nervous system and suppresses appetite in the human being. Despite the sense of happiness and the extra energy it creates, cocaine is an addictive alkaloid. Raising, possessing, or selling cocaine is illegal in almost all parts of the world. Cocaine was not discovered until 1855 in Germany: chemical research had not progressed enough before then, and transportation hardships made delivery of coca leaves in good condition from South America a real struggle. Starting from the late nineteenth century, cocaine has become a well-known recreational drug. The introduction of « crack » cocaine, with peak sales on poor inner-city markets, has made cocaine attain new heights of use in modern times.

27. The word thrives in the passage is closest in meaning to
    - A. flourishes
    - B. survives
    - C. grows
    - D. soars

28. The word clustered in the passage is closest in meaning to
    - A. white
    - B. grouped
    - C. stately
    - D. developed

29. According to paragraph 1, how many yields can a coca plant farmer expect?
    - A. one
    - B. two
    - C. three
    - D. four

30. The word its in the passage refers to
    - A. chaccar
    - B. chewing
    - C. gods
    - D. communication

31. All of the following are mentioned in the passage to explain the role of the coca plant in the Indians' lives EXCEPT
    - A. the aftermath of coca leaf addiction
    - B. a vital source of body nutrients
    - C. worship and sacrifices to their gods
    - D. anesthetics for operations on patients

32. The word they in the passage refers to
    - A. huallqui
    - B. Indians
    - C. coca leaves
    - D. pouches

33. The Colombian government has offered to totally destroy the coca plants in its country to help in the fight against cocaine abuse. Based on the passage, what could the government have offered to do?
    - A. Fail to transplant young coca plants into aspis.
    - B. Sell coca leaves exclusively to the Coca-Cola Company.
    - C. Keep coca plants away from the sunlight.
    - D. Release large numbers of Eloria noyesi into the countryside.

34. According to paragraph 3, how long is a « cocada »?
    - A. one hour
    - B. one morning
    - C. one day
    - D. one year

35. Four squares ([]) indicate where the following sentence can be added to the passage.

This was no small endeavor at this point in history.
Where would the sentence best fit?

36. The word <u>devoid</u> in this passage is closest in meaning to
    A. stripped
    B. reeking
    C. full
    D. replenished

37. According to paragraph 5, why does the Coca-Cola Company purchase coca leaves from Peru and Bolivia?
    A. To add a stimulant to the beverage they produce.
    B. Because they are in the Coke recipe.
    C. To add caffeine to their Coke beverage.
    D. Because of cocaine-extraction.

38. The word <u>hardships</u> in the passage is closest in meaning to
    A. wooden boats
    B. drawbacks
    C. steamboats
    D. difficulties

39. An introductory sentence for a brief summary of the passage is provided below. Complete the summary by selecting the THREE answer choices that express the most important ideas in the passage. Some sentences do not belong in the summary because they express ideas that are not presented in the passage or are minor ideas in the passage. **This question is worth 2 points.**

The modern day use of the coca plant undermines its former importance to the Peruvian and Bolivian Indians.

*
*
*

The coca leaves are harvested, dried in the sun, and packed in bags.

As a matter of fact, the coca plant is so well-known for cocaine production that researchers from Erasmus University had to prove that Indians were not addicted to coca leaves.

The fact that Indian priests of the pre-Inca period and the Inca Empire chewed on coca leaves for religious worship was a priority for the tribe.

Cocaine was discovered in 1855, after scientific techniques had become more refined.

The Coca-Cola Company buys tons of coca leaves from Peru and Bolivia to produce their famous soft drink.

F A source of nutrients and anesthetic, the coca plant helped the Indians physically in contrast with the recreational drug it provides today.

Reading 4

The term « leadership » has been a topic of study over the years, as its definition and behavioral application have been widely discussed. What is a leader? For some, a leader is an individual or a group of people, sometimes situated in the context of family, tribe, nation, state, band, classroom, or empire, who has the power to influence followers towards a cause or a goal. However, diverse leadership behaviors can add breadth to the discussion on the subject. For instance, was Adolph Hitler, who brazenly declared himself « Führer » by law (« guide » or « leader » in German) a leader, dictator, or both? And what made him any more of a leader than a schoolteacher guiding his students through the school year? The purpose of this paper is to put forth some theories and to attempt to explain the human phenomenon called leadership.

An analysis of leadership would never be complete without mentioning a study written by James MacGregor Burns in 1978. For Burns, leadership includes certain unmistakable features. First, it is collective in that leadership confined to one person is impossible. A basic requirement for leadership is both a leader or leaders and followers. Second, leadership influences motives. Whether one person or many people, a leader causes a positive change in their lives and what pushes them to move forward. Finally, leadership goes hand-in-hand with a goal. Usually, leaders present this goal to followers and persuade them with a specific plan that they should implement together to achieve the goal.

What is a follower? It would be tempting to answer that a follower is the exact opposite of a leader. In fact, a good follower is very similar to a good leader. A follower demonstrates respect, strives toward the same common goal presented by the leader, recognizes the leader's positive intent, but most of all, is candid at all times with the leader. If he is to be a good follower, he needs to tell the truth to the leader to keep him informed at all times of the general situation. Thus, it sometimes requires just as much guts and perseverance to be a follower as to be a leader.

In another work on the subject, Ronald Heifitz described two aspects of leadership: descriptive (how leadership occurs) and prescriptive (how it should occur). The keystone of Heifitz's theories on leadership is his idea on adaptive work. Using the example of new, unknown situations and man's difficulties in adapting to them, he then named six avoidance mechanisms the human being uses to get out of these: finding scapegoats, denial, jumping to conclusions, blaming others, externalizing the enemy, and finding a distracting issue. According to Heifitz, in a presciptive leadership view, a leader would face the problem head-on and rally a community of followers to deal with the adaptation issue.

In 1960, George Terry also emphasized the influence of leaders on people so that they would fight to attain a common objective. In this vein, leadership boils down to a relationship of power between leaders and followers. The definition of a leader would be a person or persons who has the power over others to guide them toward a goal. Terry's theory thus underlines the authoritarian/submissive aspect of the relationship in which the collaborative side dwindles. If this is true, how would George Terry explain the phenomenon of followership without intentional leadership? For instance, how would Mr. Terry explain the behavior of a herd of sheep, all following without the sense of a leader?

Perhaps the most interesting observation on the subject of leadership appears in Demonic Males: Apes and the Origins of Human Violence, by Richard Wrangham and Dale Peterson. [] This study reveals that among all the creatures in the animal kingdom, only humans and chimpanzees share a relentless behavior tending towards violence, territoriality, and unity behind one chief male in the group. [] They also point out that humans have inherited 98 % of their genes from the ancestors of the chimpanzees, so the two are very close in species, unlike bonobos. [] So, a viable conclusion would be that leadership is innately linked to the make-up of the human's genetic code. []

Glossary

- scapegoat: victim bouc émissaire

40. The word breadth in the passage is closest in meaning to
    - A. insight
    - B. interest
    - C. depth
    - D. light

41. The word brazenly in the passage is closest in meaning to brazenly = boldy
    - A. boldly
    - B. suddenly
    - C. impulsively
    - D. instantly

42. What is the aim of this report?
    - A. To prove that man's leadership is directly commensurate to the construction of his genetic code.
    - B. To define the concepts of leadership and followership.
    - C. To explain George Terry's theories on leadership and power.
    - D. To theorize and extrapolate ideas on human leadership.

43. The word them in the passage refers to
    - A. lives
    - B. people
    - C. motives
    - D. leaders

44. How do James MacGregor Burns and George Terry differ in their theories on leadership?
    - A. They agree that leaders motivate people towards a common goal.
    - B. They differ on the goals that are pursued.
    - C. They do not concur on the relationship between leader and follower.
    - D. They underscore followership without intentional leadership.

45. All of the following are mentioned in the passage to characterize a follower EXCEPT
    - A. Determination and fortitude
    - B. Unified to a goal
    - C. Regard for the leader
    - D. Withholding feedback

46. The word these in the passage refers to
    - A. adaptations
    - B. difficulties
    - C. mechanisms
    - D. theories

47. In which of the following chapters would George Terry's theory most probably appear?
    - A. Unintentional leadership
    - B. Leadership and collaboration
    - C. The plight of leaders
    - D. The authority of the leader

48. The word <u>dwindles</u> in the passage is closest in meaning to
    A. shrinks
    B. hounds
    C. rebukes
    D. increases

49. Four squares ([]) indicate where the following sentence can be added to the passage.
    These other monkeys, bonobos, a more remotely related species to man, do not rally behind the chief male of the group.
    Where would the sentence best fit into the passage ?

50. The word <u>relentless</u> in the passage is closest in meaning to
    A. unmistakable
    B. undeniable
    C. unmerciful
    D. haughty

51. What can be inferred from paragraph 6 about chimpanzees and human beings ?
    A. Leadership can be linked to demons.
    B. Violence and territoriality have been studied in fish.
    C. Human beings are all that remains of ancient chimpanzees.
    D. Chimpanzees are united behind one chief male human.

52. Directions : Complete the table by matching the phrases below.
    Directions : select the appropriate phrases from the answer choices and match them. This question is worth 3 points. Drag your answer choices to the spaces where they belong. To remove an answer choice, click on it.

Answer choices	*A descriptive leader*
1. A committed member of the Women's Club Welcome Committee	*
2. A fresh water fish which adjusts to salt water	*
3. A charismatic blue collar worker who volunteers for the company union	*
4. An aspiring Chief Executive Officer struggling to save jobs	*
	A descriptive leader
5. A new coach on a hockey team	*
6. A sheepdog with a herd of sheep	*
7. A nominee detailing a plan for the whole community	*
8. A male chimpanzee who has marked his territory	*

2. Listening section

Directions

The Listening section measures your ability to understand conversations and lectures in English. Each conversation or lecture will be heard only one time. After listening, you will answer questions about what you have heard. Answer the questions based on what is stated or implied by the speakers.

You are allowed to take notes while you listen and may use them to help answer the questions.

When you see this icon  it means you will hear part of the conversation or lecture again.

Some questions have special directions. Most of the questions are worth one point. For questions worth more than one point there will be special instructions indicating how many points you can receive.

You must answer each question. After answering, click **Next**, then **OK** to confirm your answer and go to the next question. After clicking on **OK**, you will not be able to return to previous questions.

You will have 20 minutes to answer the questions in this section. This does not include time spent listening. A clock at the top of the screen displays how much time is remaining. The clock will not count down while you are listening to test material.

Note: In the Listening Section of the official TOEFL iBT, you will both hear and read the questions.

Listening text #1 – Earth Sciences

NARRATOR: Now get ready to answer the questions. You may use your notes to help you answer.

1. What is the main topic of this lecture?
   A. Global Warming.
   B. Cloud Types and Characteristics.

C. Current Research on Clouds.
D. The Role of Clouds in Climate Change.

2. Match the characteristic with the type of cloud. Click on the type of cloud and then in the box where it belongs. This question is worth two points.

Cirrus *Cumulus* *Stratus*	
Have a cauliflower-like appearance	Cumulus
Are the highest clouds at 30,000 feet	Cirus
Feathery, fibrous appearance	Cirus
Gray and thick	Stratus

3. Listen again to part of the lecture. Then answer the question.
(Le texte est entendu mais pas vu sur l'écran.)
«Oh, by the way.....Dew point....is defined as the temperature the air would have to be cooled to in order for saturation to occur....and Saturation is when the air is holding the maximum amount of water vapor possible at the existing temperature and pressure. But I am getting off track here....... Other ways that clouds are formed are by a reduction of pressure aloft or by the mixing of warmer and cooler air currents.»
Why does the professor say this:
«But I am getting off track here.......»
A. to indicate that she is nearing the end of the lecture.
B. to let the students know that she has just given some information outside of the scope of the planned lecture.
C. to remind herself that she is running out of time.
D. to correct what she just said.

4. Which of the following is true about clouds and global warming?
A. As the climate warms there will be more clouds.
B. All theories predict that clouds will reduce the amount of surface warming.
C. Clouds will not be a central part of climate change.
D. Computer models cannot predict how clouds will react.

5. Which of the following is <u>not</u> mentioned as an element of a cloud's composition?
A. Water vapor.
B. Ice crystals.

C. Liquid water droplets.
D. Snow crystals.

6. According to the lecture, what are two ways clouds form ? This question is worth two points.
Click on 2 answers.
A. As the result of the maximum amount of water vapor present in the air.
B. When there is a reduction of pressure aloft.
C. When surface heat causes air to rise.
D. When warmer and cooler air currents mix.

Listening text #2 – Conversation Financial aid

NARRATOR : Now get ready to answer the questions. You may use your notes to help you answer.

7. What is the man's problem ?
A. He is unsure about changing his major.
B. He needs help finding a job.
C. He needs help with his tuition.
D. He wants to take a semester off.

8. What does the woman suggest that the man do now ?
A. Fill out the forms for a student loan.
B. Come back next year.
C. Get a summer job.
D. Apply for monthly tuition payments.

9. Listen again to part of the lecture. Then answer the question.
(Le texte est entendu mais pas vu sur l'écran.)
« Well, I can tell you that both of those majors are very well endowed »
What does she mean by this ?
A. She means that these are both interesting fields of study.
B. She is showing approval of these two majors.
C. She means that financial aid is available for both these majors.
D. She means that both these majors are popular with students.

10. Number the steps in applying for Financial Aid through the College. This question is worth two points.

STEPS	*Number 1-4*
1. Determine student's eligibility.	3
2. Student/parents fill out FAFSA.	1
3. Financial aid package offered to eligible student.	4
4. SAR sent out to college and financial aid agencies.	2

11. Which of the following is <u>not</u> a requirement to be considered for Tuition Deferment?
    - A. A GPA of 4.0.
    - B. Financial need.
    - C. Attendance at the college for at least one year.
    - D. Good academic standing.

Listening text #3 – Business Plan

NARRATOR: Now get ready to answer the questions. You may use your notes to help you answer.

12. What is the main topic of this lecture?
    - A. The way businesses adapt to a changing environment.
    - B. The reasons why established businesses need a business plan.
    - C. The content of a business plan.
    - D. How to differentiate a new product on the market.

13. Listen to part of the recording again. (Le texte est entendu mais pas vu sur l'écran).

    «Good.....glad to see you have all done your reading assignment!» **(RECORDED)**

    Why does the professor say this?
    - A. She is ironic, and is expressing her displeasure that the students do not know what was in the assignment.
    - B. She is letting the students know that they did well on the test.
    - C. She is showing her approval that the students are answering the question correctly.
    - D. She is reacting to seeing all the students reading their textbooks.

14. What does the professor say is the main difference between a business model and a business plan?
    × A. A business plan is long and detailed whereas a business model is short and concise.
    B. Business plans are only needed for new businesses.
    C. Business plans are for investors and business models are for the business owners themselves.
    D. A business plan is a legal document but a business model is not.

15. Which of the following elements are mentioned by students as being elements of a business plan? **This question is worth two points.**

Element	*Part of business model – yes or no*
Product positioning	X
Pricing	X
Market segment	X
Loans	
Competitive studies	

16. Who is the main audience for a business plan/business model?
    A. Customers
    B. Press
    × C. Investors
    D. Employees

Listening text #4 – Child Development

NARRATOR: Now get ready to answer the questions. You may use your notes to help you answer.

17. What is the main topic of the talk?
    A. Developmental delays.
    × B. Acquisition of speech and language.
    C. Developmental milestones for children.
    D. The difference between receptive language and expressive language.

18. Indicate whether the following are examples of receptive language or expressive language:

	Receptive	*Expressive*
Understanding sounds		
Picking out mother's voice		
Written language		
A baby's crying		

19. When is the most progress in speech and language made?
    A. Before birth.
    B. Soon after birth.
    C. Between two and five years of age.
    D. During the first year.

20. Listen again to part of the lecture.
    Then answer the question.
    « Language, on the other hand – is much broader. It encompasses the reception and expression of information. There are two parts to speech – I'm sorry, to language. »
    Why does the professor say this:
    « I'm sorry, to language. »
    A. She does not agree with the statement.
    B. She is correcting what she said previously.
    C. She anticipates that the students will not like this fact.
    D. She has mispronounced a word.

21. According to the lecture, what are two of the milestones at 5-6 months? Click on 2 answers. **This question is worth two points.**
    A. Recognize their own names.
    B. Make cooing sounds.
    C. Babble.
    D. Wave bye-bye.

22. What are the two most common causes of speech delay? Click on 2 answers.
    A. Hearing loss.
    B. Autism.
    C. Mutism.
    D. Cerebral Palsy.

Listening text #5 – Renaissance

NARRATOR: Now get ready to answer the questions. You may use your notes to help you answer.

23. What is the main topic of this lecture?
    - A. The Art of the Renaissance.
    - B. The English Renaissance.
    - C. The Social and Economic context of the Renaissance.
    - D. The Cultural Patrons of the Renaissance.

24. Which of the following are mentioned as factors that led the European Economy into Recession in the 14th Century? **This question is worth two points.**

Mentioned as a factor?	*Yes/No*
Relocation of the Papacy to France	
Change in climate	
Hundred years war	
Florin becoming the main international currency	
Expansion of the Ottoman empire	
The Black Death	

25. Listen again to part of the lecture. Then answer the question.
    (Le texte est entendu mais pas vu sur l'écran.)
    « Our goal is to lead up to the study of the art of the Renaissance. But what was happening politically and socially during the Renaissance and in the time leading up to it? »
    Why does the professor say this?
    « But what was happening politically and socially during the Renaissance and in the time leading up to it? »
    - A. He is addressing a question to the class.
    - B. He is reviewing a previous statement.
    - C. He is introducing the subject of the lecture he will give.
    - D. He is being ironic.

26. Which of the following were elements of the Renaissance?
    Place a check mark next to those that were.

Literature	
Agriculture	
Classical art	
Classical Greek works	
Architecture	

27. What is the professor's attitude about the study of Renaissance art?
   A. It must be understood in its social and political context.
   B. It is an extremely complex subject.
   C. It is difficult to understand.
   D. It took place in a vacuum.

28. When did the Renaissance start?
   A. The early 1300s.
   B. The 15th century.
   C. The 16th century.
   D. The 14th century.

Listening text #6 – conversation – class

NARRATOR: Now get ready to answer the questions. You may use your notes to help you answer.

29. What is mentioned as counting for 30 % of the final grade?
   A. The term paper.
   B. The final exam.
   C. Class participation.
   D. Homework.

30. Listen again to part of the conversation and then answer the question. **(Le texte est entendu mais pas vu à l'écran)**.
   « The section has been a great complement to the lecture. We have talked in-depth about a lot of the material and really gotten into some of the underlying theory. »
   What is the « section » the woman is referring to?
   A. The small group meeting that is held each week after the lecture.
   B. A group of students who get together to study.
   C. Students who are being tutored by a grad student.
   D. A particular part of the classroom where students go for extra help.

31. What does the man suggest that the woman do?
    A. Start studying for the final exam.
    B. Write a longer term paper.
    C. Meet with her T.A.
    D. Study with other students.

32. What is the main reason for the woman coming to talk to her Professor?
    A. She cannot find a topic for her term paper.
    B. She does not know how to study for the final exam.
    C. Her T.A. was unable to clarify the calculation for the final grade.
    D. She is hoping to get an extra-credit assignment.

33. From the conversation, where are they in the semester?
    A. The beginning of the semester.
    B. A few weeks into the semester.
    C. Heading towards the end of the semester.
    D. At the very end of the semester.

3. Speaking section

Directions

In this section of the test you will answer six questions by speaking into the microphone. Answer each of the questions as completely as possible. (**NOTE: On this diagnostic test, your answers will not be recorded.**)

You may take notes while reading and listening to the conversations and lectures. You may use your notes to help prepare your response.

Listen carefully to the directions for each question. The directions are not shown on the screen.

For each question you will be given a short time to prepare your response. A clock will show how much preparation time is remaining. When the preparation time is up, you will be told to begin your response. A clock will show how much response time is remaining. A message will appear on the screen when the response time has ended.

Speaking#1 – Independent Speaking

Preparation time : 15 seconds

Response Time : 45 seconds

Think of a teacher who has had an influence on you. Describe the qualities this teacher possessed and in what way he or she influenced you. Provide details and examples to support your explanation.

Speaking#2 – Independent Speaking

Preparation time : 15 seconds

Response time : 45 seconds

Some students prefer to study for final exams on their own and others prefer to attend group study sessions. Which do you think is better and why ?

Speaking #3 – Integrated Speaking

NARRATOR : Read the following article from a college newspaper about proposed plans for the expansion of the college library. You have 45 seconds to read the passage. Please begin reading now.

The university library needs to be expanded and the Regents are examining various proposals for the new structure. One idea that is being considered is joining forces with the city and building a new combined University/Public library on the site of the present-day University library. The advantages will be a larger collection, an increased operating budget and longer opening hours. Those who oppose the joint venture say that the increased traffic on and around campus will cause parking problems and traffic jams, and that the library will be more crowded and possibly noisier.

Narrator : Now listen to a student who is speaking at a student forum about the proposed joint library.

Narrator : The student expresses her opinion about the university's proposal for a library. State her opinion and explain the reasons she gives for holding that opinion.

Preparation time : 30 seconds

Response time : 60 seconds

Speaking#4 – Integrated speaking

Narrator: Now read the passage about social class. You have 45 seconds to read the passage. Begin reading now.

The importance and definition of class varies over time and between societies, but it impacts people, the lives they lead, and the opportunities they have access to.

The term social class was first used in the early 19th century. The most influential early theories of class were those of Karl Marx and Max Weber. Weber's theory was made up of three components, with social, status and party classes as distinct elements. Marx's theory focused on the interplay between the dominant class and the serving class.

Narrator : Now listen to part of a lecture on this topic in a sociology class.

Narrator: The professor describes the changes in the concept of class and its characteristics in the 20th century. Explain the main changes and give examples.

Preparation time: 30 seconds

Response time: 60 seconds

Speaking #5 – Integrated speaking

Narrator: Now listen to a conversation between a student and her friend.

Narrator: The students talk about two possible solutions to the woman's problem. First describe the problem and then say which of the two solutions you prefer and why.

Preparation time: 20 seconds

Response time: 60 seconds

Speaking #6 – Integrated speaking

Narrator: Listen to the description of cell phone plans.

Narrator: Using points from the talk, explain the decisions facing a new cell phone user

Preparation time: 20 seconds

Response time: 60 seconds

4. Writing section

Integrated Writing – Writing Task 1

Directions

You have 20 minutes to plan and write your response. Your response will be judged on the basis of the quality of your writing and on how well your response presents the points in the lecture and their relationship to the reading passage. Typically, an effective response will be 150 to 255 words.

Reading passage

October 12, 1492 is a widely recognized date, and Columbus Day is still celebrated in many countries in the Americas today. Christopher Columbus brought many things back to the Spanish court on his ship, including gold, the unknown tobacco plant, turkeys, pineapples, and a few Indians. However, on his trip back to Europe, when he saw mountains in Cuba, he was convinced that these were the Himalayas of India. He was still unaware that he had not gone to Asia during his trip.

The journal that Christopher Columbus kept is most explicit about many aspects of the new encounter between Old and New worlds. He first refers to the conversion of native Americans as his primary motive: « As I saw that they were very friendly to us, and perceived that they could be much more easily converted to our holy faith by gentle means than by force, I presented them with some...strings of beads... » He then observed that the Indians « seemed to be a very poor people », all completely naked. He also commented that the Indians had no weapons, even cutting themselves on swords « through ignorance ». He thought the Indians « would be good servants » and intended to bring back six natives « to teach them our language ». On the whole, Columbus was pleased by his first sight of native Americans, because he writes « All whom I saw were young, not above thirty years of age, well made, with fine shapes and faces, their hair short, and coarse like that of a horse's tail » and repeats his many praises throughout his journal.

Many critics believe that Christopher Columbus wrote with such awe of the Indians in his journal that he originated the myth of the « noble savage ». In any case, upon leaving the New World, it is clear that his intentions were to return and trade on friendly terms with the Indians.

Lecture

Now, listen to part of a lecture on the topic you just read about.

Question

Summarize the points made in the lecture you just heard, explaining how they cast doubt on points made in the reading.

Independent Writing – Writing Task 2

Read the question below. You have 30 minutes to plan, write, and revise your essay. Typically, an effective essay will contain a minimum of 300 words.

Question

Do you agree or disagree with the following statement?

The most important aspect of higher education is the door it can open to a good job in one's future life.

Use specific reasons and examples to support your answer.

TROISIÈME PARTIE

PREPAREZ-VOUS AUX QUATRE EPREUVES DU TOEFL IBT

CHAPITRE 4

Préparez-vous à la Reading section

1. Tableau diagnostic
2. Les questions de linguistique
3. Compréhension du texte et des détails
4. Construction du texte

Cette section du TOEFL iBT comprend de trois à cinq textes d'environ 700 mots, suivis de douze à quatorze questions chacun. Comme il y a un temps limité de soixante à cent minutes, cela fait une minute et demie environ par question, sans compter le temps de lecture. Cela veut dire qu'il est quasiment impossible de lire les textes lentement et en détail.

Il faudra donc avoir acquis la capacité de parcourir rapidement un texte académique en anglais, d'en tirer les idées majeures, et de revenir sur certains détails.

Mais il faut aussi savoir que tout le texte ne pourra s'afficher en entier à l'écran. Il faudra savoir manier l'ascenseur et la souris de l'ordinateur pour pouvoir faire dérouler le texte assez rapidement. Il faut également avoir l'habitude de faire un glisser-déplacer avec la souris pour certaines questions.

Les auteurs du TOEFL iBT ont annoncé eux-mêmes que les textes à l'examen seraient de nature académique, du même style que ceux étudiés dans les universités américaines.

Il est évident que plus vous lisez, mieux vous vous préparez. Mais il vaudrait mieux choisir de lire des magazines ou des journaux sérieux, comme Time ou Newsweek ou, mieux encore, l'encyclopédie. Ce dernier conseil peut vous sembler étrange, mais le style des textes soumis à l'examen ressemble tout à fait à ceux d'une encyclopédie.

Si vous n'avez pas accès à une encyclopédie en anglais, consultez www.wikipedia.org régulièrement pour vous entraîner.

Il faut aussi vous préparer au style des questions posées à l'examen.

Vous avez sûrement passé le test diagnostic. Consultez le tableau qui suit pour mieux analyser le style de questions que vous aurez à affronter le jour du TOEFL iBT et pour repérer celles qui vous posent problème.

1. Tableau diagnostic

Le tableau ci-dessous vous permettra de repérer les différentes difficultés sur lesquelles vous devez travailler.

Type de question	Numéro des questions correspondantes dans le Diagnostic Test
Linguistique	
La signification du vocabulaire	1, 4, 6, 9, 14, 17, 20, 27, 28, 36, 38, 40, 41, 48, 50
La paraphrase	19
Compréhension du texte et des détails	
Les antécédents	2,16, 30, 32, 43, 46
Les exceptions	11,25, 31, 45
La compréhension	3, 5, 7, 8, 10, 15, 18, 21, 23, 24, 29, 33, 34, 37, 42, 44, 47
Les sous-entendus	51
Construction du texte	
Les résumés et les tableaux	13,26, 39, 52
L'insertion d'une phrase	12,22, 35, 49

2. Les questions de linguistique

La signification du vocabulaire

Les questions consacrées à la signification de mots de vocabulaire occupent une place importante au TOEFL iBT.

Voici quelques ficelles pour vous aider à deviner le sens d'un mot si vous ne le connaissez pas.

Mots de référence dans le texte

Certaines phrases comportent des mots qui se réfèrent à un autre mot, dans la même phrase. Ces mots de référence peuvent se situer n'importe où dans la phrase. Savoir reconnaître un ou plusieurs mots de référence permet souvent de découvrir la signification d'un autre mot.

After the accident, the fisherman's limb was put into a cast, and Mat was told to go back to the leg doctor in one month.

Le premier indice dans cette phrase est le mot « cast », qui indique que Mat porte un plâtre. Cependant, le mot de référence, « leg doctor » est le meilleur indice pour réussir à définir le mot limb, qui, dans ce contexte, veut dire « jambe ».

Constructions de phrase

On peut s'appuyer parfois sur la construction de la phrase. Il y a plusieurs constructions de phrase où l'on peut trouver des indices pour deviner le sens d'un mot qu'on ne connaît pas.

La première construction est **l'exemple**, déclenché par un des mots suivants :

Des mots qui annoncent l'exemple	
As	Like
For example	Next
For instance	Such as
Including	Thus

Exemple

Household pets such as dogs, cats, and birds, are forbidden entry for hygiene reasons.

Dans cette phrase, si l'on ne sait pas ce que c'est qu'un « pet » en anglais, on a quelques exemples qui illustrent le mot « Dogs, cats, and birds » et aident à une généralisation pour arriver à la signification « animal domestique ».

La deuxième construction de phrase est **le contraste**. En exprimant une idée opposée, la phrase peut inclure des indices pour deviner le sens d'un mot. Voici des mots qui déclenchent l'usage du contraste :

Des mots qui annoncent le contraste	
But	Instead
Despite	Or
However	Unlike
In contrast	Whereas
In spite of	

Exemple

The Hawaiian hibiscus, state flower of Hawaii, thrives in warm climates, whereas it cannot survive in snowy winter climates.
Si cette fleur ne supporte pas un climat froid en hiver, alors le mot « thrives » dans le contexte d'un climat chaud veut dire, par opposition, « prospérer, bien vivre ».

La troisième construction est l'usage de plusieurs **catégories de conjonctions** :

to thrive = prosperer bien vivre

Rajout	Contradiction	Cause et effet
Also	Although	Consequently
And	But	Hence
Besides	However	So
Furthermore	Nevertheless	Therefore
Moreover	Still	Thus
	Yet	

Le premier groupe implique un rajout avec deux parties de phrase qui se renforcent.

Le deuxième groupe implique la contradiction avec deux parties de phrase en opposition.

Enfin, le troisième groupe indique en première partie de la phrase une cause et en deuxième partie un effet.

Ces conjonctions peuvent être utiles pour mieux interpréter le contexte de la phrase et par conséquent, déceler le sens des mots de vocabulaire recherchés.

Exemples

Regardez les exemples suivants :
Our hotel was sleazy moreover even the shower didn't work.
Many students thought that Gaetan was holding a grudge against his teacher after he received his bad report card, yet he continued to bring her an apple every day.
The movies enticed Ellie, hence she moved to Hollywood.
Dans le premier cas, les deux propositions liées par moreover sont équivalentes. Si la douche ne marchait pas, on peut deviner que l'hôtel était « de mauvaise qualité ».

Le deuxième exemple comprend deux propositions en opposition. Si Gaetan offre une pomme à sa maîtresse tous les jours, contrairement à ce qui se passe dans l'autre partie de la phrase, on peut deviner que « to hold a grudge » veut dire « tenir rancune à quelqu'un ».

Enfin, dans le troisième exemple, Ellie a déménagé à Hollywood à cause du cinéma et donc on peut deviner que « to entice » veut dire « attirer ».

Les préfixes, les racines, et les suffixes

Même si les listes de préfixes et de suffixes peuvent sembler interminables et que passer son temps à les apprendre tous par cœur n'est pas forcément une méthode efficace pour réussir au TOEFL iBT, en connaître certains peut dépanner lorsqu'on cherche le sens d'un mot sans avoir aucun indice dans la phrase.

Voici quelques exemples qui illustrent le rôle des préfixes, des racines, et des suffixes :

Préfixes	Sens	Racines	Sens	Suffixes	Sens
Ad-, as-	À, vers	Duct	Mener	Acy, -cy	Etat ou qualité
Ambi-	Les deux	Gress	Bouger	-Age	Activité
Con-, com-, co-	Ensemble, avec	Ject	Jeter	-Al	Action
De-	De, vers le bas	Pel, pulse	Pousser	-Ee	Personne affectée
E-, ex-	A l'extérieur	Quire	Chercher	-Ful	Quantité
Extra-	Au-delà de	Sentio	Sentir	-Hood	Status
In-	Dans	Soro	Soeur	-Ify	Cause
Inter-	Entre, parmi	Spect, spec	Regarder, voir	-Ism	Attitude
Re-	Encore, de retour	Vene, vent	Venir	-Ship	Status
Semi-	Moitié	Vis	Voir	-Y	Résultat d'une activité

EXERCICE 1 : la signification du vocabulaire à partir des préfixes, des suffixes, et des racines

Consigne : reliez chaque mot de vocabulaire à gauche avec sa définition à droite.

F 1. Expel
I 2. Inquiry
J 2. Ambidextrous
H 4. Semicolon
G 5. Ingress
E 6. Sorority
B 7. Accuracy
K 8. Dejected
D 9. Interject
L 10. Resentful
A 11. Conduct
C 12. Repel

A. Behavior
B. Concentration on details
C. To push away
D. To exclaim
E. Association for college women
F. To throw out indefinitely
G. Means of entering
H. Punctuation mark
I. Information search
J. Using both hands
K. Discouraged
L. Looking for revenge

(Correction au chapitre 10)

Il va de soi que ces méthodes pour comprendre grâce au contexte sont parfois insuffisantes, mais elles donnent les moyens d'avancer au lieu de rester au point zéro.

EXERCICE 2 : Révision de la signification du vocabulaire

Consigne : encerclez le sens des mots soulignés suivants.

1. <u>Impinging</u> on secretaries is a practice that's as old as the hills, including asking them to stay late, having them make coffee and paying them low wages.
   A. Bossing
   B. Taking advantage of
   C. Managing
   D. Hiring

2. With the <u>advent</u> of Christmas, shopkeepers put decorations in their store windows.
   A. driving
   B. seeking
   C. coming
   D. sight

3. Snow <u>hindered</u> the Maine potato farmers from putting down fertilizer in May this year, thus they only spread some light insecticide in June.
   A. hampered
   B. avoided
   C. omitted
   D. postponed

4. Each time those workers have a <u>grievance</u>, they go to their foreman to discuss their demands.
   A. sorrow
   B. question
   C. doubt
   D. complaint

5. Wearing certain clothing has never been condoned by public schools, yet anything is better than required uniforms.
   A. criticized
   B. promoted
   C. approved of
   D. questioned

6. A number two pencil is compulsory for any computer-corrected exam, with a good eraser besides.
   A. advised
   B. mandatory
   C. voluntary
   D. useful

7. Instead of providing immediate relief, going to the hospital did not necessarily alleviate Jack's pain right away.
   A. soothe
   B. cause
   C. worsen
   D. levelize

8. When a student is eighteen years old, one blunder can cause a complete change in his future and in his career plans. Consequently, a future nurse might have to settle for a lesser-paying job.
   A. stroke of luck
   B. surprising event
   C. serious mistake
   D. lie

9. The Benjamin Johnson case ended this evening with a hung jury. Besides, all the evidence presented for the last three weeks was flimsy.
   A. decisive
   B. genuine
   C. weak
   D. extravagant

10. In order to better understand its target audience, the Russet Company has decided to conduct a survey on toothbrushing habits in adults over 40 years old.
   A. collect
   B. follow
   C. condemn
   D. run

(Correction au chapitre 10)

La paraphrase

Au TOEFL iBT, une des façons de tester la compréhension est le choix de la paraphrase : « dans le texte » une phrase apparaît en gras. Dans « la question », il faut choisir entre quatre propositions de paraphrases celle qui a le même sens que la phrase en gras.

Les questions en paraphrase peuvent tester la compréhension des antécédents, des expressions en anglais, ou le vocabulaire.

Voici un exemple d'une mauvaise paraphrase, à cause d'une confusion d'antécédents :

Phrase 1 : Gustave Flaubert, whose female character, Mrs. Bovary, exemplified the boredom of country living, depicted her as insecure and unable to cope with her situation.

Paraphrase : Mrs. Bovary exemplified the boredom of country living and was depicted as insecure and unable to cope with her situation by Gustave Flaubert, his female character.

La confusion d'antécédents dans cet exemple est évidente.

Lorsqu'il s'agit de vocabulaire ou d'expressions en anglais, l'art de la paraphrase peut devenir plus compliqué.

Voici un exemple d'une mauvaise paraphrase, à cause d'une confusion de vocabulaire :

Phrase 1 : Instead of being astonished that eating shark is akin to eating steak, only more tender, Roland reveled in it.

Paraphrase : Roland revealed how his dietary habits had drastically changed by eating shark steak.

Il n'est pas difficile de repérer une erreur de vocabulaire : « to revel » dans la première phrase veut dire « prendre plaisir » tandis que « to reveal » dans la deuxième veut dire « dévoiler ».

Dans la première phrase, Roland mange du requin pour la première fois et apprécie son goût. Dans la deuxième, il dévoile que le steack de requin fait partie de son régime. Les deux phrases n'expriment pas la même idée.

EXERCICE 3 : La paraphrase

Consigne : encerclez la paraphrase qui a le même sens que la phrase modèle.

1. Polar bears, which live in northwestern Canada, have been observed to demonstrate sporadic mating behavior due to growing numbers of visitors to that region.
   A. Northwestern Canadians have been observed to demonstrate sporadic mating behavior due to growing numbers of polar bears to the region.

B. Only northwestern Canadian polar bears have been observed as demonstrating sporadic mating behavior due to growing numbers of visitors to that region.
C. Visitors to northwestern Canada have been observed as behaving sporadically in demonstrations when mating near polar bears.
D. It has been observed in northwestern Canada that polar bears, which live there, mate sporadically because of an increasing number of visitors.

2. Elementary schoolteachers, who usually are not doctoral graduates in Education, are nonetheless able to reliably teach a range of subjects to their students by demonstrating forbearance in choosing proper textbooks and ignoring others.
   A. Even though elementary schoolteachers are not doctoral graduates, they practice principles of Education on their students through their patience in proper textbook choices and rejection of unuseful ones.
   B. Elementary schoolteachers neither have doctorates in Education nor teach a range of subjects to their students because they do not know how to choose textbooks in a trustworthy manner.
   C. Elementary schoolteachers, who usually are not doctoral graduates in Education, have other forbearing teachers take their class because they are ignorant.
   D. Elementary schoolteachers, who usually are not doctoral graduates in Education, nevertheless trustfully teach a range of subjects to their students by ignoring them.

3. Scientific authorities have been reluctant to support the hypothesis of some researchers that earthquakes occur faster near young mountain chains, like the Himalayas, than on old faults.
   A. Scientific authorities support the researchers' views about earthquakes occurring in young mountain chains.
   B. Researchers have found that scientific authorities are not in favor of earthquakes occurring in the Himalayas.
   C. Some researchers have found that earthquakes take place more often near young mountain chains than old ones, but this has not been completely accepted by scientific authorities.
   D. According to researchers and some scientific authorities, earthquakes are brought about less often near old faults than near young mountain chains.

(Correction au chapitre 10)

3. Compréhension du texte et des détails

Les antécédents

Le TOEFL iBT demande au candidat de trouver l'antécédent de certains pronoms ou adjectifs, en spécifiant le paragraphe où ils se trouvent. Ces questions forcent le candidat à lire des phrases en détail, et donc à ralentir sa lecture, dans le contexte d'un examen à temps limité. Voici les mots qui peuvent comporter des antécédents :

Pronoms personnels	
Subject	Object
He, she, it, they	Him, her, it, them
Pronoms relatifs	
Who, whom, which, that, whose	
Adjectifs possessifs	
His, her, their, its	

Il faut surtout prendre le temps de bien examiner les quelques mots ou phrases qui précèdent le pronom ou l'adjectif. Car le piège, c'est que plusieurs mots précèdent le pronom ou l'adjectif et que tous pourraient servir d'antécédents. Il faut donc un temps de réflexion pour choisir l'antécédent correct.

EXERCICE 4 : Les antécédents

Consigne : encerclez l'antécédent correct (du mot souligné)

1. The Polish astronomer, Copernicus, found a new order for our solar system, based on the paper he wrote which described the Earth as not located in the center. <u>It</u> also named the correct order of the known planets and analyzed in detail the causes for the seasons.

   A. center C. order
   B. premise D. astronomer

2. Small farmers in the Plain states wished that they were able to express their ideas with more clout to the United States government rather than rely on plantation owners to influence the law. <u>Their</u> plan for crop efficiency remained unheard last week.

A. owners
B. states
C. ideas
D. farmers

3. Even cooks who know how to make a baked Alaska sign up for lessons in this well-known school, whose diploma is internationally recognized and whose entrance standards are very high.
A. school
B. diploma
C. lessons
D. cooks

4. Psychology claims that children who have been through several ordeals during their formative years may be influenced during their teens. As a matter of fact, they can have lasting effects for life.
A. children
B. ordeals
C. years
D. teens

5. Jimmy Connors says a tennis champion should never falter at a crucial moment. His job requires perseverance even up until match point.
A. champion
B. Jimmy Connors
C. moment
D. falter

(Correction au chapitre 10)

Les exceptions

La recherche de l'exception, force, elle aussi, le candidat à lire dans le détail, et donc plus lentement.

D'habitude, tous les quatre éléments de réponse figurent dans le texte, on ne peut donc rien éliminer sans une lecture attentive.

Exemple

Voici une question type :
Henry Wadsworth Longfellow, born in Maine, has become famous today for numerous poems he wrote. Among these are The Song of Hiawatha and Paul Revere's Ride. He studied at Bowdoin College where he became both a librarian and a professor of languages. This was after a three-year European tour between 1826 and 1829. Longfellow ended his life in Boston as a professor at Harvard. In 1906, a bridge was named after him in that city.

The author specifies all of the following as Longfellow's work EXCEPT

A. librarian C. poet

B. tour guide D. professor

Dans ce texte, on observe que Longfellow a effectué un tour de l'Europe entre 1826 et 1829, mais rien ne spécifie qu'il a été lui-même guide. Il faut néanmoins retenir que le mot « tour », tel qu'il figure dans le texte, peut induire le candidat en erreur.

EXERCICE 5 : Les exceptions

Consigne : encerclez l'exception correcte.

1. Being a friend goes beyond the status of acquaintanceship with another human being. Friendship entails sharing each other's company, demonstrating loyalty, utmost respect, and mutual esteem. There is usually a sense of helping each other, whether through exchange of advice or sharing through bad times.
 The author mentions all of the following as qualities of friendship EXCEPT
 A. acquaintanceship C. loyalty
 B. respect D. esteem

2. Blood is composed of plasma, red cells, white cells, and platelets. It plays an important part in the human body in that it removes waste (carbon dioxide), supplies nutrients (oxygen), and transports substances (amino acids). The average adult has a blood volume of approximately 5 liters or 7 % of the human body weight.
 All of the following are functions of blood EXCEPT
 A. waste removal C. nutrient supply
 B. white cell supply D. substance transport

3. The twentieth century will have seen numerous discoveries but none as prominent as the infamous hole in the ozone layer, observed in 1985 in Antarctica. Scientists were immediately alarmed by this finding, for even though ozone is just one element of the Earth's stratosphere, it does act as an important protector against the sun and its untraviolet rays. The result of a lack of protection from these harmful rays is skin cancer, eye disease and damage to marine life, as well as crop destruction and environmental pollution.
 The author mentions all of the following as effects due to a thinned ozone layer EXCEPT

A. harm to plants
B. sight problems
C. curbed protection from the sun
D. an alarming stratosphere

(Correction au chapitre 10)

La compréhension

Les questions de compréhension qui figurent au TOEFL iBT sont variées et sans forme particulière. Si la question se réfère à une idée précise dans le texte, le paragraphe correspondant sera signalé et fléché.

Pour être à l'aise dans cette section de l'examen, il faut avoir la capacité à parcourir des textes scolaires en anglais et avoir atteint un niveau de lecture équivalent à celui du niveau universitaire américain.

Les sous-entendus

En revanche, les questions à sous-entendus (en anglais, « inference questions ») sont souvent les mêmes et peuvent se préparer à l'avance.

Lors de la lecture d'un texte, on peut s'apercevoir que certains éléments ne sont pas détaillés explicitement, mais que le lecteur peut les déduire à partir d'autres données dans ce texte.

Exemples

Refrigerators with a flash defrost feature are more popular with the elderly population than classic ones because they cut down on maintenance work.

Mis à part ce qu'on peut apprendre au sujet des réfrigérateurs auto-dégivrants dans cette phrase, on peut faire d'autres suppositions sur les réfrigérateurs classiques. Tout d'abord, par opposition à la popularité des réfrigérateurs auto-dégivrants, on peut déduire que les frigos classiques sont moins populaires parmi les personnes âgées. Ensuite, on peut aussi comprendre que l'entretien des frigos classiques est plus lourd que celui des frigos auto-dégivrants.

Voici un autre exemple :

Texel, the largest of the islands located between the Dutch mainland and the West Frisian Islands, accommodates more than 300 species of birds, including the Eurasian spoonbill and other migratory birds. Texel ranks among the largest breeding grounds in Europe.

What can be inferred from this paragraph about Texel?

A. The Eurasian spoonbill is a native bird of Texel.
B. The Eurasian spoonbill is an aquatic bird.
C. The Eurasian spoonbill migrates to Texel to mate.
D. Texel is a famous Dutch resort for birds.

En lisant le mot « Eurasian », on déduit que l'oiseau vit en Europe et en Asie. Les mots « and other migratory birds » indiquent qu'il s'agit d'un oiseau migrateur qui voyage entre ces deux endroits. Puisqu'un grand nombre d'oiseaux se reproduisent à Texel, on déduit que c'est là que le spoonbill eurasiatique s'accouple. La bonne réponse est la C.

EXERCICE 6 : La compréhension et les sous-entendus

Consigne : répondez aux questions qui suivent les textes.

The average American knows little about the Constitution and the powers its authors delegated during the eighteenth century. The power to tax was put on Congress's shoulders, although the President presents the annual budget. Despite this separation of power, the Congress often amends the President's suggestions for taxation and budget and demonstrates its upper hand granted by the Constitution. It is beyond a doubt that the Constitution favors the legislative branch over the executive. In modern times, however, with the world becoming smaller through travel and communications, power in general has fallen into the hands of single heads of government, whatever their educational background or titles might be.

1. What can be inferred from this text about the evolution of power?
   A. It has continued in the spirit of the Constitution.
   B. It has moved to the President.
   C. It has tilted the balance in favor of the Congress.
   D. It has shifted to individuals.

2. The major idea of this paragraph deals with
   A. the power of the Constitution.
   B. the power of the President.
   C. the balance of power.
   D. the power of the Congress.

3. In which of the following chapters would this passage most probably appear?
   A. Specific activities of Congress.
   B. Specific activities of the President.
   C. Specific activities of heads of government.
   D. Historical interpretations of the Constitution.

Each school year, students must submit applications if they want to receive financial aid. Deadlines must be met early, even before dates for school application. A student asking for federal or state monies must clearly justify his claims in a written statement, a legal prerequisite adopted by most MBA schools.
Students may use the Financial Aid Form (FAF) which is published by the College Scholarship Service (CSS) of the College Board to apply for financial aid. Many schools have also accepted the needs analysis service of the Graduate and Professional School Financial Aid Service (GAPSFAS).

4. A written statement must be made by
   A. MBA applicants
   B. legal applicants
   C. the Graduate and Professional School Financial Aid Service
   D. financial aid applicants

5. What can be inferred from this text about financial aid?
   A. It is granted to most MBA students.
   B. It is granted to students who have met early deadlines.
   C. It is a legal prerequisite.
   D. It is granted to students who wish to receive funds.

6. « A legal prerequisite », as it is mentioned in this passage
   A. applies to all MBA students.
   B. is published by the College Scholarship Service.
   C. is valid for all students desiring state money.
   D. is valid for all applicants for financial aid.

7. Students wishing to apply for financial assistance may
   A. use an application form published by the GAPSFAS.
   B. submit to the MBA school.
   C. precede application deadlines.
   D. use the FAF.

8. We know the following about the College Scholarship Service:
   A. They establish deadlines.
   B. They counsel students on financial Matters.
   C. They publish standardized applications.
   D. They are a part of the GAPSFAS.

(Correction au chapitre 10)

4. Construction du texte

Les résumés de texte et les tableaux

The Educational Testing Service, auteur du TOEFL iBT, classe en trois catégories les raisons pour la lecture de textes académiques :

1) reading to find information

2) comprehension

3) reading to learn.

Les questions qui se rapportent à la reconnaissance de l'organisation du texte font partie de la troisième catégorie. Elles vont au-delà d'un simple repérage de détails dans le texte. Pour pouvoir y répondre, il faut savoir parcourir un texte d'environ 700 mots en retenant les éléments majeurs et les détails importants.

Chacun s'est confronté au résumé de texte à l'école, où l'on apprend à hiérarchiser les idées essentielles et secondaires. Ici, il s'agit du même exercice, mais à la suite d'une simple lecture. Il vaut mieux lire le texte une fois en entier pour repérer l'idée générale, de manière rapide et efficace. Ensuite, il faut savoir aller à l'essentiel, sans perdre de temps sur les exemples.

Quant aux tableaux, il s'agit de les compléter grâce au même repérage des idées essentielles d'un texte : il faut donc lire et comprendre les idées essentielles d'un texte et ensuite pouvoir les mettre en application en complétant un tableau à leur sujet.

L'exercice suivant vous propose un entraînement au résumé de texte à partir de textes courts. Si vous avez du mal à faire cet exercice, vous devriez revoir vos cours de français à propos des résumés de texte.

EXERCICE 7 : Les résumés de texte et les tableaux

Consigne : Dégagez trois idées essentielles pour chacun des deux textes suivants.

1. Advertising can be classified as a means of communication, therefore it stands to reason that communication is the basic source for stating advertising goals. Experts express their goals clearly, such as « When a survey is taken and consu-

mers make a list of brands they know in one product range, 30 % of these people will mention our brand». It is clear that these goals can be checked by survey, and they usually remain valid for a certain period of time.
Advertising goals, however, are not expressed in relation to sales. As a matter of fact, sales were historically a criterium for judging the effects of advertising, but now experts have changed their outlook on selling. In their new opinion, sales are not just a result of advertising, but of other things. Thus, the emphasis is now put on communication objectives.

1.
2.
3.

2. Have you been looking in the mirror these days and not liking what you see? Gray hair – pull it, cut it, tint it – it still grows in, due to a variety of genetic reasons. If your parents or grandparents turned gray early, despair! You will probably turn gray at the same age, in the same pattern, because of heredity. If you are Caucasian, tough luck! The average black sees his first gray hair at 44 years old, while Caucasians have a head start at 34.
What to do? It may surprise you to know that all the hair follicles you will ever have were intact three months before your birth. And while your hair may be vibrant, it is really a non-organic material with the same proteins found in fingernails. In fact, destiny and nature seem to be against us!

1.
2.
3.

(Correction au chapitre 10)

L'insertion d'une phrase

Au TOEFL iBT, on rencontre également des questions où il faut insérer une phrase. Quatre carrés figurent dans le texte, à la fin de quatre phrases successives, d'habitude dans le même paragraphe.

La question, qui figure après le texte, propose une phrase qu'on est censé insérer au bon endroit. Il faut donc trouver le bon paragraphe et ensuite choisir une des quatre positions pour l'insérer à l'endroit le plus logique.

Exemple

Voici un exemple de ce type de question :
Most people wishing to decorate eggs select only white ones at their grocer's counter and hard boil them in an enamel, stainless steel or glass pot. ☐ In order to obtain an even color, it is important to pour one tablespoon of vinegar into an 8 oz. container before dropping a color tablet in. ☐ After adding 1/2 cup cold water, the egg is dunked for a minimum of three minutes until the desired shade is obtained. ☐ The drying time is usually ten minutes, unless wax decorations have been applied before the color phase, which lengthens the process. ☐

Dans ce paragraphe, les quatre carrés correspondent aux quatre endroits où l'on peut insérer une nouvelle phrase.

Maintenant, observons des phrases à insérer, avec plusieurs critères.

La première phrase est la suivante :

An ideal choice would be an old-fashioned Paul Revere sauce pan.

Le mot « sauce pan » est un synonyme exact de « pot », et veut dire « casserole ». Cette phrase tombe donc dans la catégorie d'exemples, parce qu'elle illustre le type de casserole qu'on peut utiliser pour bouillir les œufs à décorer. Il faut donc l'insérer après la première phrase, parce qu'un exemple suit toujours son antécédent.

La prochaine catégorie, cause et effet, est illustrée par la phrase suivante :

Leaving the egg in the dye for a good ten minutes will enable you to obtain deep purple and Navy blue.

La troisième phrase du paragraphe précise que l'œuf est trempé pendant un minimum de trois minutes jusqu'à l'obtention de la teinte de couleur souhaitée. Par extension de cette idée, on peut faire tremper l'œuf pendant dix minutes pour obtenir du mauve ou du bleu foncé. Il faut donc l'insérer après la troisième phrase, parce qu'elle suit la même idée de cause et effet.

Enfin, observons l'insertion de phrase chronologique. Voici l'exemple :

Decorators should allow at least half an hour before peeling the wax to obtain their designs in white.

L'unique phrase du texte dans laquelle on mentionne la cire est la dernière (« wax decorations »). Cette phrase est donc insérée à la fin du texte, pour compléter l'explication de cette démarche.

EXERCICE 8 : L'insertion d'une phrase

Consigne : Insérez la phrase en gras au bon endroit.

1. In the year 2000, computer manufacturers issued profit warnings, and computers were staying on shelves.☐ Some people believed that the market was saturated and that it would be hard to sell computers to people with little money or to those who didn't need them. ☐ People were also buying cheaper but efficient computers because companies were offering substantial discounts on their entire range of items, including their best sellers. ☐ This meant that prices were lower, so profits were smaller. ☐
   Look at the four squares (☐) that indicate where the following sentence could be added to the passage.
   One company, Apple, even offered a rebate on its star product.
   Where would the sentence best fit?

2. Although toy sales have ups and downs, the Barbie doll, invented in the 1950's by Mattel, America's biggest toy maker, is still a success. ☐ In 1993, she celebrated her 35th birthday, with 775 million dolls sold. ☐ Barbie's success is due to Mattel's continual diversification of the product. ☐ The average American girl owns eight Barbie toys, and Barbie is sold in 31 different countries. ☐
   Look at the four squares (☐) that indicate where the following sentence could be added to the passage.
   The Barbie doll can be bought with different careers, boyfriend, friends, and accessories.
   Where would the sentence best fit?

3. Temporary staff used to be seasonal, because their main role used to be replacement for permanent workers during their summer holidays. ☐ However, times have changed, and temporary workers help companies reduce labor costs. ☐ Companies have a core of permanent staff which is their fixed labor cost. ☐ To

complement these workers, temps are hired when necessary to work at times when the company needs them. □

Look at the four squares (□) that indicate where the following sentence could be added to the passage.

If there is a sudden big need for productivity, a company can then rely on temporary staff without having to pay them fixed salaries or signing long-term contracts.

Where would the sentence best fit?

(Correction au chapitre 10)

CHAPITRE 5

Préparez-vous à la Listening Section

1. Listening dans les autres parties du TOEFL iBT
2. Les questions
3. Comment préparer cette partie
4. Les signaux dans le langage
5. Comment prendre des notes en écoutant une conférence
6. Comment prendre des notes en écoutant une conversation

La partie *Listening* du TOEFL iBT est complètement nouvelle par rapport aux versions antérieures du TOEFL. Nous estimons que les changements sont très positifs. Les conférences et les conversations qui sont présentées dans cette partie de l'examen sont très proches de ce que vous entendrez dans une université américaine. Ce qui veut dire que la partie *Listening* du TOEFL iBT est un très bon moyen de juger le niveau d'un étudiant français qui veut faire ses études aux Etats-Unis. Et c'est un très bon moyen pour vous de vous faire une idée du niveau d'anglais qu'il faut avoir pour poursuivre vos études dans une université américaine. En vous préparant au *Listening*, gardez en tête cette idée : c'est un échantillon de ce qui vous attend aux États-Unis !

Commençons par résumer ce que comprend la partie *Listening*:

	Longueur	**Nombre**	**Nombre de questions**
Conférence	3 à 5 minutes ; 500 – 800 mots	4 à 6	6 questions par conférence
Conversations	3 minutes	2 à 3	5 questions par conversation

Les conférences se présentent soit comme des cours magistraux, soit comme des séquences interactives avec des étudiants qui posent des questions ou qui répondent aux questions. Elles portent sur les différents sujets étudiés à l'université.

Les conversations peuvent être entre deux étudiants, un étudiant et un professeur, ou un étudiant et une autre personne du milieu universitaire. Elles portent sur des sujets liés à la vie universitaire ; le travail de classe, les devoirs, les démarches administratives, le logement, les bourses, etc.

La partie *Listening* mesure votre capacité de comprendre l'anglais parlé d'Amérique du nord et d'autres pays anglophones. A chaque examen, l'un des exposés est prononcé avec un accent anglais ou australien.

Les conférences et les conversations que vous entendrez sont plus longues et la langue est plus naturelle que dans les versions précédentes du TOEFL. C'est vraiment la langue telle qu'on l'entend tous les jours. Il y a des pauses, des hésitations, quelquefois l'interlocuteur se corrige ou revient sur un mot.

1. Listening dans les autres parties du TOEFL iBT

Rappelez-vous qu'il y a des textes à écouter dans trois parties du TOEFL iBT ; la partie *Listening*, la partie *Speaking*, et la partie *Writing*.

Listening	Integrated Speaking	Integrated Writing
Il faut répondre aux questions (QCM et autre). En conséquence, il faut essayer de bien saisir les points principaux et secondaires et même les nuances.	Listen/Speak : il faut donner un résumé de ce que vous avez entendu ou bien expliquer le sujet et donner votre avis. Vous pouvez vous concentrer sur les points qui seront importants pour le résumé ; pas forcément des détails. Read/Listen/Speak : il faut faire un résumé de ce que vous avez entendu/lu en expliquant les liens entre le texte écouté et le texte écrit.	Vous écrivez un résumé de ce que vous avez entendu en expliquant le rapport avec ce que vous avez lu dans le texte.

Vous avez le droit de prendre des notes en écoutant les enregistrements. Heureusement, car certains exposés durent jusqu'à cinq minutes.

Pour certaines questions, une partie de la conférence ou de la conversation est repassée avant que vous entendiez la question.

Les tâches ont les buts suivants :

1. La compréhension générale :

Comprendre l'idée principale, les points principaux, et les détails importants liés à l'idée principale.

La compréhension de tous les détails n'est pas nécessaire.

2. La compréhension pragmatique

Identifiez l'attitude ou le degré de certitude de l'interlocuteur.

Identifiez la fonction ou le but de l'interlocuteur.

3. Lier et synthétiser l'information :

Reconnaître l'organisation de l'information.

Comprendre les rapports entre les idées présentées (comparer et contraster, cause et effet, ou les étapes dans un processus).

Tirer des conclusions fondées sur ce qui est impliqué dans le matériel.

Faire des liens entre des différentes informations dans une conversation ou une conférence.

Reconnaître des changements de sujet, exemples, et digressions dans des conversations et des conférences. Reconnaître des introductions et des conclusions dans des conférences.

2. Les questions

Il y a quatre types de questions dans la partie *Listening*:

1. Des QCMs avec quatre choix et une seule bonne réponse.
2. Des QCMs avec plus d'une bonne réponse.
3. Des questions où il faut mettre en ordre les étapes d'un processus ou d'un événement.
4. Des questions où il faut aligner des réponses avec des catégories dans un tableau (diagramme).

Pour réussir la partie *Listening*, il faut savoir prendre des notes en écoutant la conférence/conversation. Vous ne pouvez pas dépendre de votre mémoire pour répondre aux questions, car les exposés durent jusqu'à cinq minutes. Il faut pouvoir noter les idées principales, etc. pour les consulter ensuite.

Les digressions

Il y a souvent des digressions dans les conférences que vous allez écouter. En anglais, elles s'appellent des « asides ». Attendez-vous à des questions sur ces digressions. Il faut pouvoir les identifier et comprendre leur sens.

Exemples de digressions

I would say that was the most important reason for the loss of the election. **Oh, and don't forget to hand in your papers on Friday.....**

Now if there are no questions on the discovery of Penicillin, let's move on to how it was used. **In any case, if you take the 2nd part of the course next semester, you will study the chemical composition of Penicillin more in detail.**

We are now half way through our study of the Crusades. **That reminds me; make sure you review for next week's test.**

This would make a good subject for a thesis. **It's always a good idea to start thinking about a specialization for graduate work......**now let's look at the theory behind it.

We will be covering that material Friday. **Personally, I would cancel class that day but the department voted not to.**

3. Comment préparer cette partie

D'abord, il faut vous confronter au problème de la compréhension. Si vous ne comprenez pas bien ce que vous entendez, votre première réaction sera d'essayer d'écrire tout ce que vous arrivez à comprendre. Evidemment, ce serait impossible car le débit de mots sera au moins cinq fois plus rapide que votre vitesse d'écrire. Si vous avez des problèmes de compréhension, il faut beaucoup y travailler avant le jour « J ».

Si vous ne comprenez pas bien, vous essaierez de noter mot à mot ce que vous pensez avoir entendu. Mais vous ne pouvez pas prendre des notes mot à mot, faute de temps. Il faut paraphraser. En plus, la tentation avec une prise de notes mot à mot, pour la partie *Speaking,* est de répéter ces mots dans votre enregistrement, alors que cela n'a pas de sens.

Comment faire pour travailler la compréhension orale? Il n'y a qu'un seul moyen : écouter, écouter, écouter… tout ce que vous pouvez, en anglais. Plus vous vous entraînerez à entendre l'anglais, mieux vous comprendrez. Si vous avez accès à la télévision par câble, essayez de trouver des programmes qui ressemblent à une conférence d'université. Par exemple, des programmes sur l'actualité, des débats, entretiens, etc. Cela vous donnera une expérience plus proche de celle du TOEFL iBT que des séries télévisées ou des films.

Une fois que vous commencerez à vous sentir plus à l'aise en écoutant l'anglais, commencez à vous entraîner à prendre des notes. Il faut commencer par écouter une émission et simplement prendre des notes. Mais au fur et à mesure que vous progresserez, il serait très utile de pouvoir réécouter l'émission pour revoir vos notes et travailler votre méthode. Vous pouvez enregistrer des émissions ou bien utiliser des CDs des méthodes d'anglais, au niveau avancé.

Des conseils pour vous aider à prendre des notes

Dans la majorité des cas, c'est dans les premières phrases de son exposé que le conférencier va présenter le sujet et sa spécificité.

Les premières phrases vont vous donner des indices importants pour la structure et le contenu de ce qui va suivre. Ces renseignements peuvent vous aider à avoir une structure dans votre tête, ce qui vous aidera à prendre des notes de manière plus organisée et plus utile.

La conclusion d'une conférence contient souvent un résumé de ce qui a été dit et vous aide à retrouver des idées principales que vous n'avez pas eu le temps de noter auparavant. Si vous avez un doute, la conclusion peut aussi vous aider à clarifier vos idées et gagner un temps important.

Vos notes devraient être un résumé des idées principales et secondaires, et des liaisons entre ces idées. Il faut écrire avec discernement, en choisissant avec soin ce que vous allez noter, car vous avez un temps très limité pour écrire. En plus, si vous réfléchissez trop sur une phrase vous allez manquer la suite et vous vous perdrez. Si vous essayez d'écrire ce que vous entendez mot à mot, c'est perdu d'avance.

Utilisez des abréviations à chaque fois que c'est possible pour écrire plus vite. Ne faites pas attention à l'orthographe, car l'important est de reconnaître le mot après l'avoir écrit. Il vaut mieux écrire, par exemple, skolarship, que de réfléchir trop longtemps à l'orthographe correcte de ce mot (scholarship).

N'écrire qu'en anglais. Si vous notez en français, vous allez perdre un temps précieux à faire la traduction. De toute façon, si vous ne comprenez pas un mot en anglais mais comprenez le sens de la phrase, l'écriture en français ne vous avancera pas.

Laissez de l'espace entre des lignes pour pouvoir rajouter une idée ou un détail qui est lié à ce que vous avez déjà écrit. Par exemple, si le conférencier fait référence à trois idées secondaires dans son introduction et que vous les écrivez sur une ligne, quand il faudra ajouter des détails, vous devrez réécrire ces trois idées secondaires, ce qui vous fera perdre du temps.

Voir ci-dessous, à titre d'exemple – si vous aviez écrit chaque nom d'auteur sur une ligne différente dès le début, vous n'auriez pas à les réécrire. Ne vous inquiétez pas de gaspiller du papier – laissez de la place pour y revenir plus tard au cours de l'exposé et ajouter des idées liées à ce que vous avez déjà écrit.

Writers of classic juvenile fiction – Twain, Alcott + Wilder
Shared themes – family, adventure, moral choices
Twain – masc. Protagonists working class
Alcott – female prot., bourgeois
Wilder – autobiographical

Si vous n'utilisez pas cette façon de faire, vous allez essayer de revenir sur vos notes et rajouter plus entre les lignes, ce qui rendra la lecture très difficile.

Essayez d'anticiper ce que le conférencier va dire grâce à des indices de l'introduction. Cela vous aidera à prendre des notes, car vous pourrez suivre plus facilement.

Faites attention aux indices verbaux qui signalent une idée importante (voir liste plus loin).

Essayez de comprendre la structure de l'exposé. Voici les structures les plus communes :

Ordre de temps —
- Par chronologie
- Par cause et effet
- Par processus

Ordre de classification – divisant quelque chose en catégories ou pièces qui la constituent.

Ordre de définition – donnant les caractéristiques de différentes choses.

Ordre de Comparaison/Contraste – donnant les similarités ou les différences entre deux choses.

4. Les signaux dans le langage

Un conférencier va utiliser des signaux verbaux pour introduire des idées importantes et pour structurer son sujet. Si vous connaissez ces expressions et ce qu'elles veulent dire, il vous sera plus facile de suivre.

Voici des mots et des phrases clés qui annoncent l'organisation du sujet dans la conférence :

Introduction du sujet

Today we will be discussing……..
Today we will be examining…..
We will be exploring…..
We will be looking at…….
Our subject today is……
There are x reasons why…….
Our focus is on………

Ou bien on va droit au sujet :
The painters heralded as the Impressionists brought about a complete change in the world of painting.
Imagine the world before vaccinations existed. A world where 3 children out of 5 died of a childhood disease.

Les idées principales

Most importantly.....
One of the main reasons.....
One of the critical reasons......
A major development.....
A central reason....
An essential factor....
First and foremost....
The focus of.......

Les idées secondaires

In addition
Other important reasons/factors/
Similarly...
Also.....
Furthermore....
In the same way...
For example....
For instance...
.... also contributed to.........
We must also take into account.........
.... also accounted for..........

Les contrastes

However
But
Despite
In spite of
On the other hand
Conversely
Contrary to what we might think
On the contrary
Similarly

Les conclusions et les résumés

Therefore
As a result
The conclusion being that….
To conclude….
To summarize….
To recap….
Finally…..
In conclusion…
In other words….
To put it another way….
Therefore…
As we have seen….
Consequently…
In brief
To wrap up
For these reasons

Les points importants

Now this is important….
The important thing here is…..
I want to stress that…..
I want to emphasize that….
Remember that….
Keep in mind that….

Les causes et effets

Consequently
Therefore
If… then….
As…..then
Accordingly
Because

5. Comment prendre des notes en écoutant une conférence

Nous allons examiner comment prendre des notes en écoutant une conférence.

Dès la première phrase, il faut repérer les indices qui annoncent le sujet et la structure de la conférence. On peut alors structurer sa feuille de notes dès le début pour pouvoir mieux comprendre à la fin. En plus, dans la partie *Listening*, on a un temps assez court pour répondre aux questions. Moins on passe à rechercher des réponses dans ses notes, mieux c'est.

Sur le CD-ROM joint à ce livre, il y a une conférence intitulée « Practice listening: Industrial Revolution ». Pour commencer, écoutez-la et prenez des notes.

Maintenant que vous avez fait une première tentative, regardons de près chaque paragraphe de l'exposé pour voir comment prendre des notes plus efficacement.

Commençons avec le premier paragraphe :

Today we are starting our study of the Industrial Revolution. Now, to set things straight... let's be clear on this... there were two Industrial Revolutions. The first Industrial Revolution took place in Great Britain at the end of the 18th century. The second began at the end of the 19th century in the United States. I'll give some background on the British Industrial Revolution, but my main focus will be on the American version.

Vous pourriez structurer vos notes par rapport à ce premier paragraphe qui explique le déroulement de la conférence :

Industrial Revolution GB 18th C	USA – 19th C

Si vous divisez votre feuille en deux, en attribuant à la partie gauche les notes sur la première révolution industrielle en Grande-Bretagne, et à la partie droite les notes sur la deuxième révolution industrielle aux États-Unis, vous avez un format qui vous permet d'ajouter des notes sans avoir à noter chaque fois la référence.

Ici, vous avez pu repérer les deux grandes lignes de l'exposé, en remarquant que le sujet principal est la révolution industrielle aux Etats-Unis.

Continuons à prendre des notes sur le deuxième paragraphe :

The Industrial Revolution refers to economic and social changes which were the result of the introduction of new technologies of production. The Industrial Revolution brought about a major shift in society – before it occurred societies were essentially agricultural; after the Industrial Revolution society was dominated by industry and manufacturing. The consequences were both positive and negative, as we shall see.

Industrial Revolution GB 18th C Change from agricultural to mfg. Society – pos + neg.	USA – 19th C

L'important est ici le passage d'une société reposant sur l'agriculture à une société fondée sur l'industrie, avec des effets à la fois positifs et négatifs. Cela est valable pour les deux pays – vous pourriez donc l'écrire au milieu de la page, comme cela, à la relecture, vous saurez que cette remarque est valable pour les deux pays.

The British Industrial Revolution followed the rapid adaptation of three new technologies – the steam machine, which used coal, machines for spinning thread and weaving cloth, which were driven by steam, and furnaces to make iron ore into finished metal, also using coal.

GB 18th C Shift from agricultural to mfg. society – pos + neg. Due to use of 3 new tech : Steam machine – coal driven Spinning and weaving – steam Furnaces – coal	USA – 19th C

Dans ce paragraphe, on veut retenir les causes de la révolution industrielle en GB. **Donnez le nom des nouvelles technologies et celui des énergies qui ont permis le fonctionnement des nouvelles machines.**

There were three major developments responsible for the 2nd Industrial Revolution. The most important one was the completion of modern transportation and communication networks. These were railroad, steamship, telegraph and cable. The second one was the advent of electricity in the 1880s. Widespread electricity made many things possible – power, urban transportation, better illumination in the workplace and the home. The third development was the application of science to industrial processes.

GB 18th C Shift from agricultural to mfg. society – pos + neg. Due to use of 3 new tech : Steam machine – coal Spinning and weaving – steam Furnaces – coal	USA – 19th C 3 dev. : Completion of modern trans. + comm. Networks. RR, steamship, telegr. Cable. Widespread elec. Appl. of science to indust. processes

Ici, on veut noter les trois développements responsables pour la deuxième révolution industrielle.

In 18th and 19th century England there was plenty of skilled labor so the new machines did not replace workers, rather the machines made work more efficient. In America the growing nation had an inadequate work force and so machines helped to supplement it.

GB 18th C Shift from agricultural to mfg. society – pos + neg. Due to use of 3 new tech : Steam machine – coal Spinning and weaving – steam Furnaces – coal Adequate labor – machines added efficiency	USA – 19th C Innovations in prod. Of metals, machinery, chemicals + food 3 dev. : Completion of modern trans. + comm. Networks. RR, steamship, telegr. Cable. Widespread elec. Appl. of science to indust. Processes Supplemented inadequate workforce

Ici ce qu'il est important de noter, c'est la différence par rapport aux hommes – les machines ont aidé à rendre le travail plus efficace en Grande-Bretagne, où il y avait assez de travailleurs. En revanche, aux USA, les machines ont été un supplément à une main-d'œuvre trop peu nombreuse.

The second Industrial Revolution marked huge progress for industry, but the social consequences were not so bright. One of these consequences was urban growth. People left rural areas and came to cities to find work. This new working class had poor living conditions. Due to low wages children began to enter the workforce, toiling in factories alongside adults to help support their families.

GB 18th C Shift from agricultural to mfg. society – pos + neg. Due to use of 3 new tech : Steam machine – coal Spinning and weaving – steam Furnaces – coal Adequate labor – machines more efficient	USA – 19th C Innovations in prod. of metals, machinery, chemicals + food 3 dev. : Completion of modern trans. + comm. Networks. RR, steamship, telegr. Cable. Widespread elec. Appl. Of science to indust. processes Supplemented inadequate workforce Social conseq – urban growth, poor living cond., children working

L'important ici est la même chose pour les deux côtés de la feuille – les conséquences sociales de la révolution industrielle.

The effect of the Industrial Revolution on women's work is interesting to note. Before the Industrial Revolution, American women did much of the work necessary for family survival. Yarn, cloth, candles and food were manufactured by women in the home. By 1790 water-powered machinery was put into use in the manufacture of cloth, taking over from women's hand labor. Early mills increased the value of women's household labor through outwork. This refers to the practice of contracting work out to women to do at home. As late as 1820, more than two-thirds of cloth manufactured in the US was produced by women working at home.

GB 18th C	USA – 19th C
Shift from agricultural to mfg. society – pos + neg. Due to use of 3 new tech : Steam machine – coal Spinning and weaving – steam	Innovations in prod. of metals, machinery, chemicals + food
Furnaces – coal	3 dev. : Completion of modern trans. + comm. Networks. RR, steamship, telegr. Cable. Widespread elec. Appl. Of science to indust. processes
Adequate labor – machines more efficient	Supplemented inadequate workforce
Social conseq – urban growth, poor living cond., children working	Before IR yarn, cloth, candles + food made by women at home. Value of trad. Women's work increased. Outwork – women working at home mfg. 2/3 of cloth in USA 1820

Ici on peut retenir que la nature du travail féminin a changé car les tâches traditionnelles faites par les femmes à la maison étaient désormais accomplies par la machine. On note la définition du mot « outwork » – travail fait par des femmes chez elles, pour une usine.

The use of outwork declined after the first textile factory opened in Waltham Massachusetts in 1814. The success of this factory brought about the development of the urban working class and the network of single-industry towns. Lowell, Massachusetts became the leading textile center in America. The factory workers were single, white, native-born women from middle-class New England farms. They worked over 70 hours a week at low wages.

GB 18th C	USA – 19th C
Shift from agricultural to mfg. society – pos + neg.	
Due to use of 3 new tech :	
Steam machine – coal	Innovations in prod. of metals, machinery, chemicals + food
Spinning and weaving – steam	
Furnaces – coal	3 dev. :
	Completion of modern trans. + comm. Networks. RR, steamship, telegr. Cable.
	Widespread elec.
	Appl. Of science to indust. processes
Adequate labor – machines more efficient	Supplemented inadequate workforce
Social conseq – urban growth, poor living cond.,	
children working	Outwork – women working at home mfg. 2/3 of Cloth in USA 1820
	1814 – first textile factory Waltham MA. – outwork declined. Urban working class/single industry towns. Single white US-born women worked in factories

Notez les faits importants – quand, où, qui, conséquence.

Most women working factory jobs in the first decades of industrialization were single. Immigrant and working-class wives and mothers were more often outworkers. Outwork was a very exploitative form of employment. Outworkers had limited mobility and bargaining power and so were often taken advantage of by their employers who cut and withheld wages.

GB 18th C	USA – 19th C
Shift from agricultural to mfg. society – pos + neg. Due to use of 3 new tech :	
Steam machine – coal Spinning and weaving – steam	Innovations in prod. of metals, machinery, chemicals + food
Furnaces – coal	3 dev. : Completion of modern trans. + comm. Networks. RR, steamship, telegr. Cable. Widespread elec. Appl. Of science to indust. processes
Adequate labor – machines more efficient	Supplemented inadequate workforce
Social conseq – urban growth, poor living cond., children working	Outwork – women working at home mfg. 2/3 of Cloth in USA 1820 1814 – first textile factory Waltham MA. – outwork declined. Urban working class/single industry towns. Single white US-born women worked in factories Outwork exploitative – limited mobility/bargaining power. Immig./working class wives/moms

On a déjà noté le profil des travailleuses dans les usines. Ici, on note le profil des femmes faisant le « outwork ».

One of the consequences of the Industrial Revolution for women was that their traditional work in the home was devalued. « Real » labor became work that had a concrete market value. The household was seen as a place of leisure and consumption, no longer one of labor and production.

GB 18th C	USA – 19th C
Shift from agricultural to mfg. society – pos + neg.	
Due to use of 3 new tech :	
Steam machine – coal	Innovations in prod. of metals, machinery, chemicals + food
Spinning and weaving – steam	
Furnaces – coal	3 dev. :
	Completion of modern trans. + comm. Networks. RR, steamship, telegr. Cable.
	Widespread elec.
	Appl. Of science to indust. processes
Adequate labor – machines more efficient	Supplemented inadequate workforce
Social conseq – urban growth, poor living cond., children working	Outwork – women working at home mfg. 2/3 of Cloth in USA 1820
	1814 – first textile factory Waltham MA.
	Urban working class/single industry towns.
	Outwork exploitative – limited mobility/bargaining power.
	Immig./working class wives/moms
	Conseq – women's work seen as a commodity

Pour la conclusion, on veut retenir l'idée qu'une conséquence de cette révolution industrielle a été de donner une valeur marchande au travail traditionnel des femmes

Vous voyez qu'en prenant très peu de notes vous arriverez à saisir toutes les idées importantes. Vous pourriez réécouter les textes dans le Practice Test et vous entraîner à prendre des notes de cette façon.

6. Comment prendre des notes en écoutant une conversation

Le principe est le même, mais le matériel d'écoute est présenté différemment.

Dans les conversations, il y a deux interlocuteurs. Divisez votre feuille en deux et mettez le nom d'un interlocuteur à la tête de chaque colonne. En écoutant, écrivez les notes dans la colonne appropriée.

Les conversations que vous aurez à écouter concernent toujours un problème ou une situation universitaire. Elles vous aideront à vous familiariser avec le vocabulaire spécialisé de ce milieu. Voir le chapitre 8. Une fois que vous connaîtrez certaines expressions et certains noms, vous verrez que ces conversations sont assez faciles à comprendre.

Dans le CD-ROM joint à ce livre, vous trouverez « Practice conversation for note taking ». Ecoutez la conversation et prenez des notes. Après avoir fini, voyez comment améliorer votre méthode.

D'abord, divisez votre feuille en deux, un côté pour chaque interlocuteur, comme ci-dessous :

Man	Woman

Man : Hi, I'm calling about the ad you have up in the student union. Are you still looking for a roommate ?

Woman : Yes, we are. Let me explain the situation. There are three of us – 3 students – renting a house and we need a 4th. You would have your own bedroom and a shared bathroom. We're 2 women and a man right now.

Man : I see. Are you all full-time students ?

Woman : I am, but Amanda and John work part-time and go to school part-time. What about yourself ?

Man	Woman
Ad in student union	3 students – house. Own bed/shared bath. She's FT – Amanda – school/work John – "

Il y a beaucoup de détails et de questions dans les conversations. Ce qui compte, pour avoir un résumé, c'est les faits et les détails. Ici, c'est le *qui* (3 étudiants qui cherchent un colocataire pour une maison), le *quoi* (une chambre privée et une salle de bains à partager). Mettez les prénoms des deux autres colocataires en laissant la place pour écrire ce qui les concerne.

Man : I'm a full-time student and I also work on the weekends. My name is Dave Carter, by the way.

Woman : Hi. I'm Ellie Cartwright. So, where are you living right now ?

Man : Well, I'm in the dorm… since the beginning of the semester. But I'm finding that there is really a lot of noise and partying. It's really hard to study… for me. So I decided I would rather live off-campus… um… even if it means having no food service, not being as close to the library and all that. So… what I am wondering is….how quiet is it at your place ? I mean, are you guys pretty studious ? Or do you party a lot ?

Man	Woman
Ad in student union Dave Carter Dorm – noisy. Can't study	3 students – house. Own bed/shared bath. She's FT – Ellie Cartwright Amanda – school/work & John – "

Ici, ajoutez les noms des interlocuteurs. Notez le « pourquoi » – Dave veut partir de son logement universitaire car c'est trop bruyant.

Woman : Wow, it's so hard to even get a place in the dorm… and you want to give yours up ! I understand though, all that noise would make me nuts. I can tell you that in this house we are all really serious. This year, we have had a couple of parties on the weekends, but we all have to agree on that. I'm pre-med and I have a huge amount of work. Amanda is an engineering major, so ditto. And John is a grad student and he….um… he's hoping to finish his thesis this year. So we really hit the books most of the time.

Man : That sounds good. Could you tell me a little more about the arrangement. Like how is the rent split, and the utilities. What about meals – are they group style or every man for himself ?

Man	Woman
Ad in student union Dave Carter Dorm – noisy	3 students – house. Own bed/shared bath. – lots of studying – have to agree on parties She's FT – Ellie Cartwright. Pre-med. Amanda – school/work. Engineering. & John – " – grad student.

Ici on note les domaines d'étude de chacun. Remarquez que les questions posées par Dave vous préviennent de ce qu'il va falloir noter en écoutant les réponses.

Woman : Well, we split the rent four ways as we each have our own bedroom. Utilities, the same. We have had some common meals….it's kind of fun…. but we have pretty different eating styles, so we tend… usually… to just fend for ourselves.

Man : What about cleaning? I have to say I'm pretty neat and clean…

Woman : Well, that is sometimes an issue. We assigned chores at the beginning of the year… but… well, sometimes they don't get done. We hold house meetings once a week, you know, to discuss any problems… and that has come up several times. I'm not sure how we are going to handle it.

Man : How far is the house from campus?

Woman : About 20 minutes by foot. Umm… what is your major and what year are you in?

Man	Woman
Ad in student union Dave Carter – neat/clean. Dorm – noisy	3 students – house. Own bed/shared bath. – lots of studying – have to agree on parties. Rent/utilities shared equally. Eat separately. Chores. House meeting 1x/wk. 20 mn/foot from U. She's FT – Ellie Cartwright. Pre-med. Amanda – school/work. Engineering. & John – " – grad student.

Ici, on a appris que la propreté est importante pour Dave. Les colocataires partagent le loyer et les charges équitablement, mais chacun s'occupe de ses repas et de quelques tâches ménagères. Ils tiennent une réunion une fois par semaine. La maison est à 20 minutes à pied de la fac.

Man : I'm a Sophomore, Economics. I transferred from State.

Woman : OK. You sound like a good match. Well, if you're interested… why don't you come by tonight? Uuummm… could you bring your student body card? We just want to make sure that we really have a fellow student as a roommate. With the housing shortage a lot of working people are looking to rent rooms, too. We really prefer a student.

Man : Oh, OK. Sure. So how does the interview process work? I mean, how do you decide who to accept as a roommate?

Woman : Well, we all meet you… together…. and then you can ask whatever questions you have… we'll show you the house… and then we'll ask some questions… you know, to see if we all seem compatible. Then we talk it over and we'll get back to you tomorrow.

Man : OK. And when could I move in, assuming I get chosen?

Man	Woman
Ad in student union Dave Carter – neat/clean. Sophomore, econ. Dorm – noisy	3 students – house. Own bed/shared bath. – lots of studying – have to agree on parties. Rent/utilities shared equally. Eat separately. Chores. House meeting 1x/wk. 20 mn/foot from U. Visit/talk tonight. Bring ID card – proof of student. Decision tomor. She's FT – Ellie Cartwright. Pre-med. Amanda – school/work. Engineering. & John – " – grad student.

Ici, on note des détails du processus pour devenir colocataire. Dave va visiter la maison et parler avec les autres ce soir, et ils vont le contacter demain pour lui annoncer leur décision. Ellie demande qu'il apporte sa carte d'étudiant pour prouver qu'il est vraiment inscrit à la fac.

Woman : Well, the room is empty now. Our last roommate dropped out. She paid this month's rent, though… so you could start moving in as soon as you want… the month is up next week in any case. How does it work with your dorm room ? Don't you have to pay for the whole semester in advance ?

Man : Yes, but as there is a waiting list to get into the dorms, it's not a problem. They select someone and that person just reimburses me what I already paid and the room transfers over to his name.

Woman : Great. Well, see you tonight. Does 7pm work ? We're at 225 Grant Road, just off of Harley.

Man : OK, great. See you then.

Man	Woman
Ad in student union Dave Carter – neat/clean. Sophomore, econ. Dorm – noisy Waiting list for dorm – will be reim. Rent paid in adv	3 students – house. Own bed/shared bath. – lots of studying – have to agree on parties. Rent/utilities shared equally. Eat separately. Chores. House meeting 1x/wk. 20 mn/foot from U. Visit/talk tonight.7pm Bring ID card – proof of student. Decision tomor. Move in immed. 225 Grant Rd. off Harley She's FT – Ellie Cartwright. Pre-med. Amanda – school/work. Engineering. & John – " – grad student.

Les derniers détails – l'adresse de la maison, le fait que, comme il y a une liste d'attente pour vivre dans le logement universitaire, Dave sera remboursé du loyer payé en avance. Il pourrait éventuellement déménager tout de suite, s'il est pris par Ellie, Amanda et John.

Ceci n'est qu'un exemple de conversation. Comme une des personnes voulait des renseignements et l'autre personne répondait, la structure a été très simple durant toute la conversation. Evidemment, ce n'était pas nécessaire de noter les questions, il suffisait de noter les réponses. Dans d'autres types de conversations, il faut saisir le sujet et la structure pour pouvoir déterminer dès le début la meilleure façon de prendre ses notes.

CHAPITRE 6

Préparez-vous à la Speaking Section

1. Independent Speaking

- *Critères d'évaluation*
- *Comment préparer Independent Speaking #1*
- *Exemples de sujets pour entraînement*
- *Conseils de préparation*
- *Conseils pour d'efficaces tournures de phrases*
- *Comment préparer Independent Speaking #2*
- *Exemples de sujets*
- *Conseils linguistiques*

2. Integrated Speaking

- *Comment préparer Integrated Speaking Question #3*
- *Comment préparer Integrated Speaking Question #4*
- *Comment préparer Integrated Speaking Question #5*
- *Comment préparer Integrated Speaking Question #6*

3. Le choix du style de langage

Cette partie du TOEFL iBT est nouvelle. Probablement vous n'avez rien fait de semblable auparavant, sauf peut-être des examens oraux dans des cours d'anglais.

La partie Speaking est un test de votre aptitude de parler spontanément sur un sujet. Spontanément, car 15 secondes de temps de préparation ne sont pas vraiment une préparation. C'est juste un petit moment pour vous orienter avant de parler. Durant ces 15 secondes, il faut comprendre le sujet, mettre un peu d'ordre dans ses idées, et commencer à parler tout en sachant comment on veut terminer son discours.

Avec si peu de préparation, les phrases devront sortir toutes seules et c'est ainsi que votre niveau d'anglais parlé pourra être testé : soit vos phrases seront correctes et claires, soit elles ne seront pas. Au moment où vous commencez à parler et où l'enregistrement commence, vous n'avez plus de temps de réfléchir et d'anticiper, il faut parler de façon automatique. Il faut foncer.

Dans ce chapitre, on vous propose des stratégies de préparation pour cette partie. Mais le jour de l'examen, il n'y a pas de stratégie à mettre en œuvre.

Cependant, entraînez-vous le plus possible pour développer les automatismes qui vous permettront de répondre spontanément.

Les commentaires d'étudiants qui ont déjà passé le TOEFL iBT indiquent que la partie Speaking comporte une difficulté supplémentaire : tous les candidats parlent dans leur micro au même moment. Il faut donc un très grand effort de concentration pour ne pas être distrait par ses voisins. Raison de plus pour bien préparer cette partie de l'examen. Plus vous êtes à l'aise pour les enregistrements, mieux c'est !

1. Independent Speaking

Rappelez-vous que les deux premières tâches dans cette partie sont *Independent Speaking*. Ce sont des sujets qui sollicitent votre avis personnel ou votre expérience personnelle. Il n'y a pas de document à lire ou de texte à écouter.

1.1 Critères d'évaluation

D'abord il est intéressant de savoir comment la partie « Independent Speaking » est évaluée. Les notes vont de 0 à 4. Il y a trois éléments qui sont pris en compte pour l'évaluation : Delivery (débit), language use (utilisation de la langue) et topic development (développement du sujet). Voici un résumé de ce qui est évalué pour chaque élément :

Delivery

- Prononciation
- Fluidité d'expression
- Intonation
- Hésitation

Language Use

- Vocabulaire
- Grammaire
- Structure

Topic Development

- Développement et cohérence des idées
- Adéquation de la réponse par rapport à la question
- Présentation du rapport entre les idées

1.2 Comment préparer Independent Speaking Question #1

Essayons un exemple de *Independent Speaking question #1.*

Vous entendez et lisez sur l'écran :

Talk about a movie that you have seen that left an impression on you and why.

Qu'est-ce qu'il faut faire pour préparer votre réponse ?

1. Choisir un film.
2. Résumer le film ou bien expliquer un aspect qui vous a affecté.
3. Expliquer votre sentiment ou point de vue personnel sur le film.

Voyons chaque étape en détail, en oubliant provisoirement qu'on ne dispose que de 15 secondes de préparation.

1. Choisir un film

Ce n'est pas forcément un film récent. Il faut choisir un film à propos duquel vous avez quelque chose à dire. Même si vous ne vous souvenez que de quelques parties du film, si vous avez un avis fort, cela suffira. Pour cet exercice on va parler du film « The Hours ».

2. Résumer le film ou bien expliquer un aspect qui vous a affecté, voici quelques idées sur « The Hours »

- Three women characters all linked to Mrs. Dalloway
- Three different eras- women's roles different
- Themes : meaning of life, being true to oneself, relationships with others

3. Expliquer votre sentiment ou votre point de vue personnel sur le film

- Three different women at different times all confronted by the same issues
- Search for meaning in life universal
- Small moments that were intense and consequential

Ceci est le processus de recherche d'idées que vous devez employer.

Votre enregistrement donnera quelque chose comme :

One movie that really affected me was The Hours. The movie told three related stories. The connection had to do with Virginia Woolf and her book « Mrs. Dalloway ». One of the stories showed Virginia Woolf in the... ummm... process of writing the book. The next showed a traditional housewife in 1950's America, she was, ummmm... trying to adjust to being a wife and mother. The link was that she was reading « Mrs. Dalloway ». The third was about a woman in New York, in the present, who was named Clarissa, like the character in the book. She had a... ummm... non-traditional life and was going through some intense things. All three characters were struggling with finding their place in the world, and ummm... balancing what they wanted and what those around them expected. I remember thinking that these are universal struggles and that they don't always get resolved. Another point the film made was that we are always waiting for something to happen in the future, but... things are happening now and we need to be in the moment and live those things fully, instead of always waiting for something in the future.

Bien sûr, c'est très différent d'écrire un texte ou de parler à l'improviste durant 45 secondes. Avant de commencer à vous entraîner dans les conditions de l'examen, il peut être utile de faire plusieurs exercices comme ceux qui vous sont proposés ci-dessous. Cela vous aidera à acquérir le réflexe d'organiser vos pensées très vite et de suivre un plan en parlant.

Si vous n'arrivez pas à faire cet exercice, livrez-vous à un entraînement plus profond. Il faut acquérir les automatismes qui vous permettront de parler sans préparation. Faites le même exercice, mais en prenant des notes. Si vous n'arrivez pas à structurer vos idées en parlant, écrivez un texte. Mais attention ! Le but n'est pas de bien écrire un texte, mais d'apprendre comment structurer votre réponse pour pouvoir le faire dans votre tête.

Pendant votre entraînement, utilisez la « checklist » ci-dessous pour vérifier que vous avez pensé à tout ce qui est important pour votre réponse.

Checklist :

WHAT TO THINK ABOUT	CHECK IF INCLUDED
Introduction – present your subject	
Use correct phrases to introduce ideas	
Give several details, reasons or thoughts about your subject in order to answer the question	
Express your thoughts clearly	
Use appropriate language for a classroom setting	
Speak using structures you can use correctly	
Speak for the entire time allotted (45-60 seconds)	
Finish with a brief concluding sentence	

Voici quelques sujets à utiliser pour vous entraîner. Vous pouvez soit faire comme on a vu, soit faire dans les conditions de l'examen ; lire la question, vous préparer pendant 15 secondes, et parler durant 45 secondes. Si vous vous enregistrez, vous pouvez écouter votre réponse et la retravailler pour l'améliorer.

1.3 Exemples de sujets pour entraînement – INDEPENDENT SPEAKING – QUESTION 1

- Think of a class you took in high school and how it helped prepare you for college. Give examples of what you learned and how it helped you.
- Think of a trip you took that changed the way you saw the world. Explain where you went and what you experienced that had a lasting effect on you.
- Talk about a friend that has had an impact on your life. It could be a childhood friend or someone you have met recently. What qualities does this friend have and what do you appreciate about him or her?
- Why do you want to study in the US? What do you think you will gain by going to school in another country?
- What extracurricular activity did you participate in during high school? Has it helped prepare you for college? Explain how and give examples of the skills it has developed.

1.4 Conseils de préparation

- Entraînez-vous
  C'est en vous entraînant que vous allez devenir plus à l'aise avec ce type de format. Familiarisez-vous avec le type de question dans chacune des deux parties de « Listening » déjà présentées.

- Enregistrez-vous
  Si vous vous enregistrez pendant votre entraînement, vous pourrez vous réécouter et vous pouvez travailler sur l'amélioration de votre réponse.

- Chronométrez-vous
  Après vous être suffisamment entraîné pour avoir confiance, commencez à utiliser une montre. Le but est de commencer à vous rendre compte de ce que c'est que parler pendant 45 secondes. Cela vous aidera à mieux organiser votre réponse. Vous ne voulez pas être pris au dépourvu et être obligé de vous arrêter au milieu, faute de temps.

- Variez vos phrases
  Ne commencez pas chaque phrase avec « I ». Essayez de varier les phrases et utiliser des structures différentes.
- Utilisez un vocabulaire approprié
  Votre réponse doit être dans un anglais correct. Cela veut dire que des mots d'argot (slang) sont à bannir et qu'il faut aussi éviter des mots comme « like » "yeah » "you know ». Ces expressions sont courantes dans la vie de tous les jours, mais pour cette épreuve, elles sont trop conversationnelles.

1.5 Conseils pour d'efficaces tournures de phrases

Voici des phrases qui pourraient être utiles.

Pour commencer
Eviter de commencer avec « I »

A (book, movie, teacher, etc.) that influenced me was

A (book, movie, teacher, etc.) that has had an important influence on me was.....

A (book, movie, teacher, etc.) that left an impression on me was...

« The Hours » was a movie that stayed with me long after seeing it.

« The Hours » was a book that stayed with me long after reading it.

My 2nd grade teacher taught me many things that have stayed with me all these years.

Although I have many favorite movies, one that comes to mind is...

Pour donner votre avis

In my opinion...

As I see it...

My viewpoint is...

My take on this is that...

2. Comment préparer Independent Speaking Question #2

La deuxième question dans la partie « Independent Speaking » vous présente deux points de vue sur une question personnelle et vous demande d'expliquer votre préférence.

C'est une approche différente de celle de la question numéro 1.

Regardons un exemple :

Vous entendez ou lisez sur l'écran :

Some students prefer to go to college immediately after graduating from high school while others prefer to take a year off in-between to travel or work. Which do you think is a better choice and why ?

Voici le processus de recherche d'idées à suivre :

1. D'abord choisir le point de vue que vous voulez soutenir. Vous n'êtes pas obligé de présenter votre vrai point de vue ; il vaut mieux choisir celui que vous arriverez le mieux à soutenir.

– College immediately after high school graduation.

2. Pensez aux raisons pour justifier votre choix.

- used to studying, being in school
- would be easier to continue as a student now rather than come back to school later
- I know what subject I want to study – don't want to lose my enthusiasm
- friends will all be in college next year – prefer to be in school at the same time
- would like to finish my studies as quickly as possible – start working in my chosen field

Votre enregistrement donnera quelque chose comme :

If I had the choice between starting college immediately after graduating from high school or… taking a year off to travel or work, I would prefer to start college. It would be an easy transition as I am used to studying and ummm… being in an academic environment. It might be hard to get used to that again after taking a year off. I know what I want to study and so… ummm… I'm looking forward to starting college. All my friends will start college immediately after high school and I'd prefer to be in college at the same time that they are. I also would like to finish my studies as soon as possible so I can start working in my chosen profession. So, overall I think that I am ready to start college right away, and see no reason to wait.

Regardons une autre façon de répondre à la même question :

- Would be enriched by a year spent in another country traveling
- Working for a year would help pay for college
- Working would help me decide what field I am interested in pursuing
- A break after 12 years of school is probably a good thing

Votre enregistrement donnera quelque chose comme :

Taking a year off after graduating high school seems like a good idea. After 12 years straight of being a student, working or traveling could give a student some new perspectives and… ummm… maybe some new ideas on what he would like to study in college or, ummm… what field he would like to enter later on. It could also be a good thing to be independent… to see what it is like to live in another country, work and earn your living, or have to plan and budget for a long trip. It could also be a way to earn money for college. Overall, I would say that it would be very enriching to spend a year doing something else between high school and college.

Remarquez que vous n'êtes pas obligé de répondre à la première personne.

Evidemment 15 secondes ne suffisent pas de préparer votre réponse. Vous avez à peine le temps de choisir le point de vue que vous allez soutenir et penser à un ou deux arguments en faveur de ce point de vue. Vous allez de préférence faire tout cela sans écrire. Pourquoi ? Parce que vous n'avez pas le temps de faire un plan de ce que vous voulez dire. Ecrire quelques mots ne sert pas à grand-chose, surtout si écrire vous bloque sur une seule idée. En fait, dès que vous entendez la question, vous devrez faire du « brainstorming » (séance de réflexion où vous pensez à tout ce qui est lié à votre réponse, sans jugement).

Vous pensez à tous ces points en quelques secondes. Le temps qu'il faut pour les noter est du temps en moins pour penser à autre chose. Il faut garder ces points en tête en commençant à parler. Ensuite, vous devrez plus ou moins improviser votre réponse.

Si vous devez préparer cette partie en profondeur, voici comment procéder :

1. Regarder une question type et faire du « brainstorming ».
2. A partir des idées qui émergent à cette première étape, préparer un texte.

Ou bien, si vous arrivez à sauter l'étape de l'écrit :

3. A partir des idées qui émergent à la première étape, faire une préparation dans la tête, sans rien écrire.
4. Répondre à la question en parlant dans un magnétophone pendant 45 secondes.
5. Ecouter l'enregistrement et le comparer avec le texte écrit pour voir comment l'améliorer.
6. Faire un deuxième enregistrement et répéter #5.

Regardons comment faire avec la question suivante :

Some students prefer to study in the library and others prefer to study at home.

Where do you prefer to study and why ?

1. Regarder la question et faire du « brainstorming ».
Imaginez que vous préférez étudier dans la bibliothèque. Votre « brainstorming » donnera quelque chose comme :

- silent
- access to reference books
- access to computers
- nothing to do but study – no distractions

Ou bien vous préférez étudier chez vous. Alors, vos notes donneront à peu près cela :

- Comfortable at home
- Have all my supplies
- Can make coffee or tea
- Can study as late as I want

2. A partir des idées qui ont émergé de la première étape, préparez un texte.

Votre plan sera à peu près :

- Introduce your preference
- Cite the advantages with a few details
- Personalize it
- Conclude – humor, reiterate, or stress a point

Given the choice of studying at the library or at home, I prefer to study at the library. The advantages are that, first of all, the library is really quiet. There are no distractions, such as talking, phones ringing, music or television. In addition, all the reference materials I could possibly need are available at the library. Moreover, the librarian is there to help me if I cannot find the information I need. I think I have more concentration in the library than at home, because I know I am there to study and not to do anything else. And everyone else is studying too, which is sometimes a good motivation for me. The only problem is that the chairs are not always comfortable, but maybe that is also an advantage, as it would be hard to fall asleep in those chairs !

3. A partir des idées qui ont émergé de la première étape, faire une préparation dans la tête, sans rien écrire.

Pour cette étape, vous allez essayer de recréer ce que vous avez écrit dans l'étape #2. C'est-à-dire, de vous souvenir de la forme, des mots que vous avez utilisés pour introduire vos idées, etc.

C'est important de ne rien écrire dans cette étape. Il ne faut pas s'habituer à écrire un texte. L'exercice dans l'étape #2 est valable, car à force d'écrire un texte on retient l'organisation et des phrases types. Mais on ne veut pas s'appuyer trop sur l'écrit, car cette partie de l'examen n'est pas un exercice écrit.

4. Répondre à la question en parlant dans un magnétophone pendant 45 secondes.

Ici on travaille dans les conditions de l'examen. Vous parlez spontanément sur le sujet. Vous avez eu une petite préparation dans les étapes précédentes mais ici vous vous entraînez à parler spontanément.

Votre enregistrement donnera quelque chose comme :

If I had to choose between studying in the library and studying at home, I would choose to study at the library. I think… there are several advantages to studying in the library. The atmosphere is very conducive to studying. It is quiet… and… everything is available… like books, encyclopedias, computers,… and the librarian, who can help you if you need it. You can really concentrate there, not like at home. There are no phones ringing or people talking or other kinds of noise. Ummm… that is why I prefer to study at the library. I can get more done at the library than I would at home in the same amount of time.

5. Ecouter l'enregistrement et comparer-le avec le texte écrit pour voir comment l'améliorer.

En plus, vous pouvez utiliser la check-list suivante pour vérifier que vous avez pensé à tous les points importants en écoutant votre réponse :

Checklist :

WHAT TO THINK ABOUT	CHECK IF INCLUDED
Introduction – present your subject	
Use correct phrases to introduce ideas	
Give several details, reasons or thoughts about your subject in order to answer the question	
Express your thoughts clearly	
Use appropriate language for a classroom setting	
Speak using structures you can use correctly	
Speak for the entire time allotted (45-60 seconds)	
Finish with a brief concluding sentence	

2.1 Exemples de sujets – Independent Speaking – Question 2

Students in the US have the option of attending summer school. Do you think it would be beneficial to attend summer school or to take the summer off to have other experiences such as work or travel ?

High school students can take college classes during their senior year in high school. Do you think this would be a good way to prepare for college? Give reasons to support your answer.

If you had the choice between living on campus in a dormitory and living at home with your family and commuting to school each day, which would you choose? Discuss the pros and cons of your choice.

Some students prefer to go to college immediately after graduating from high school while others prefer to take a year off in-between to travel or work. Which do you think is a better choice and why?

Some students prefer to concentrate on their classes and studying while others think it is important to participate in a club or extra-curricular activity. Which point of view do you agree with and why?

2.2 Conseils linguistiques

Pour présenter votre préférence

Given the choice between… and…, I would prefer/I would choose/my choice would be/my preference would be

If I had to choose between… and…, I would prefer/I would choose

(choice) and (choice) both have advantages, but I prefer to…

Pour expliquer votre préference

The main reason I prefer… is that…

Among the advantages of… is…

One of the reasons I prefer to… is…

There are many reasons that I prefer to…

In my opinion it is better to… because…

2. Integrated Speaking

2.1 Comment préparer Integrated Speaking Question #3

Pour la question #3 vous devrez lire-écouter-parler. D'abord vous lisez un texte court sur un problème lié à l'université. Ensuite, vous écoutez un commentaire sur le même sujet. Vous devrez résumer le commentaire dans le contexte de ce que vous avez lu.

En lisant le texte vous avez une première approche du sujet. Il faut bien saisir de quoi il s'agit, en prenant quelques notes sur l'idée principale. Essayez de tirer un maximum d'informations de votre lecture.

- Quel est le sujet principal ?
- Comment se présente-t-il ? Est-ce qu'il y a un choix à faire ou une alternative à choisir parmi plusieurs ?
- Quelle est l'importance de ce sujet dans le contexte de l'université ?

Ensuite, en écoutant l'enregistrement, vous allez comprendre ce qu'il faut résumer. Prenez des notes en étant sûr de noter les détails ou les raisons à donner pour défendre votre avis.

Pour votre enregistrement, essayez de suivre le plan suivant :

- Introduire le problème et les solutions proposées
- Présenter votre avis
- Donner des raisons ou des arguments qui vont à l'appui de votre préférence

2.2. Comment préparer Integrated Speaking Question #4

Pour la question #4, vous devrez lire-écouter-parler. Le sujet est tiré d'un cours d'université. D'abord, vous devez lire un texte court sur un sujet. Ensuite, vous devez écouter un exposé sur le même sujet qui donne des exemples et plus d'informations sur le sujet.

Vous devez essayer de sélectionner les points les plus importants pour en parler dans votre enregistrement.

En prenant vos notes, essayez de noter les détails les plus importants. Pour votre enregistrement, essayez de suivre le plan suivant :

Présentez le sujet général, puis la partie spécifique sur laquelle repose l'exposé.

Donnez autant de détails que possible.

2.3 Comment préparer Integrated Speaking Question #5

Pour la question #5 vous allez écouter-parler. Cette fois, vous écoutez une conversation à propos d'un problème lié à la vie d'étudiant. Deux solutions seront proposées. Vous devrez résumer le problème et donner votre avis sur la meilleure solution.

En prenant des notes, essayez d'être explicite sur le problème et les détails des deux solutions. Vous devrez choisir une solution et expliquer pourquoi vous la préférez.

Pour votre enregistrement, essayez de suivre le plan suivant :

- Expliquer le problème
- Mentionner les deux solutions proposées
- Expliquer pourquoi vous préférez une des solutions

2.4. Comment préparer Integrated Speaking Question #6

Pour la question #6 vous allez écouter-parler. Il s'agit d'une conférence sur un concept ou un processus. Vous devrez expliquer ce concept ou ce processus en montrant que vous l'avez compris.

C'est important de comprendre assez de détails pour que votre explication ait un sens. Si c'est un processus, il faut essayer de noter toutes les étapes pour que votre explication soit complète.

Pour votre enregistrement, essayez de suivre le plan suivant :

- Présenter le processus et à quoi il sert
- Enumérez toutes les étapes, dans l'ordre
- Donnez le résultat

3. Le choix du style de langage

Un point important pour la partie *Speaking* est le choix du style de langage à utiliser ; formel ou informel. Il n'y a pas autant de différence entre ces deux styles de langue parlée en anglais qu'en français, mais il y a une différence quand même. Il y a des expressions qu'on utiliserait avec des amis, mais pas avec des professeurs ou dans un cadre professionnel. Dans les enregistrements que vous allez faire dans le cadre de l'examen, il vaut mieux utiliser le langage formel.

Dans le tableau ci-dessous, regardez quelques exemples de la différence entre la langue formelle et informelle :

FORMELLE	INFORMELLE
To hang out with someone	To spend time with someone
To be jazzed about something	To be excited about something
To be into something	To be interested in something
To freak out	To be nervous/anxious
To flunk	To fail
To ace an exam	To do really well on an exam
To pull an all-nighter	To stay up all night studying
A drag	A challenge/a hardship
A put-down	A criticism
To chill	To relax
A bummer	A sad thing
To be laid back	To be relaxed
Awesome	Great/really nice

Au début de ce chapitre, vous avez vu la réponse type pour la question « *Talk about a movie that you have seen that left an impression on you and why.* »

Maintenant, regardons la réponse écrite dans un anglais informel. Essayez de souligner les mots ou les phrases qui ne sont pas appropriés.

The movie The Hours was really cool. There were three stories that were linked. There were three chicks. One was Virginia Woolf who was a little crazy, trying to write the book « Mrs. Dalloway ». The next was a traditional housewife trying to get into being a wife and mom. She was reading the book and it was freaking her out. The third character was a lady in New York, in the present, who was named Clarissa, like the character in the book. She led a pretty way-out life and was going through some freaky things. These three characters were all trying to find themselves and get a handle on what they wanted and what those around them wanted from them. I remember thinking that was a bummer, but that is life. Another point the film made is that we are always hanging around waiting for something to happen, but we need to be in the moment, not always just waitin' for the next thing to happen.

Maintenant, regardez le même texte où les mots et les phrases trop informels ont été soulignés. Si vous n'aviez pas trouvé la plupart de ces expressions vous-même, cela vaut la peine d'y faire plus attention.

The movie The Hours was really <u>cool</u>. There were three stories that were linked. There were three <u>chicks</u>. One was Virginia Woolf who was a little <u>crazy</u>, trying to write the book « Mrs. Dalloway ». The next was a traditional housewife trying to <u>get into</u> being a wife and mom. She was reading the book and it was <u>freaking her out</u>. The third character was a lady in New York, in the present, who was named Clarissa, like the character in the book. She led a pretty <u>way-out</u> life and was going through some <u>freaky</u> things. These three characters were all trying <u>to find themselves</u> and <u>get a handle</u> on what they wanted and what those around them wanted from them. I remember thinking that was a <u>bummer</u>, but that is life. Another point the film made is that we are always <u>hanging around</u> waiting for something to happen, but we need to be in the moment, not always just <u>waitin</u> for the next thing to happen.

Maintenant, regardez de nouveau le corrigé qui a été présenté au début du chapitre, pour vous rendre compte de la différence entre les deux styles.

One movie that really affected me was The Hours. The movie showed three intertwined stories. The connection had to do with Virginia Woolf and her book « Mrs. Dalloway ». One of the stories showed Virginia Woolf in the… ummm… process of writing the book. The next showed a traditional housewife in 1950's America trying to adjust to being a wife and mother. The link was that she was reading « Mrs. Dalloway ». The third was about a woman in New York, in the present, who was named Clarissa, like the character in the book. She had a non-traditional life and was going through some intense things. All three characters were struggling with finding their place in the world and balancing what they wanted and what those around them expected. I remember thinking that these are universal struggles and that they don't always get resolved. Another point the film made was that we are always waiting for something to happen in the future but in fact things are happening now and we need to be in the moment and live those things fully, instead of always waiting for something in the future.

Exercice

Lisez la réponse suivante et remplacez les mots soulignés, qui sont trop informels, par des mots appropriés qui ont le même sens.

The movie Elephant really spooked me. It shows a typical day in high school, with all sorts of kids. There is the weird girl, the artsy-fartsy guy, the boy-crazy girls, the jock, the lovey-dovey couple.

Then, we see the kid no one likes, who sits alone at the back of the class and is spit on by everyone. What we see next is that this kid is plotting his revenge ; he and his friend are going to blow everyone's head off.

The movie is based on the Colombine shootings that occurred a few years ago. But the movie does not try to mind-read the killers or offer any explanation or anything like that. It just shows what high school is like and what some of the kids are like and then what happens. It has some stuff that is based on the real story, like the killers watching Hitler on TV and ordering guns and planning to get even. I think the movie was really spooky cuz it seemed to be saying that this could happen anywhere ; a kid could go postal and go around taking everyone out.

Corrigé

Spook – scare
Artsy-fartsy – artistic, creative
Boy-crazy – interested in boys
Jock – athlete
Lovey-dovey – in love, affectionate

Spit on – bullied
Blow everyone's head off – murder everyone; go on a shooting spree
Anything like that – anything along those lines
Stuff – elements
Spooky – scary, disturbing
Cuz – because
Go postal – go berserk, really lose it, go out of his mind
Take everyone out – murder, kill,

Exercice

Analysez les réponses aux questions suivantes. Soulignez les expressions trop informelles et essayez de les remplacer avec des expressions plus appropriées.

1. What do you like about being a student?
   It's cool being a student because you can learn a lot of interesting stuff and do fun things in your free time, like sports and stuff like that. You can find ways to travel and meet new buddies. Sometimes you get stressed out, like about grades and stuff like that, but most of the time it's pretty fun.
2. Talk about a difficulty you encountered in the past year and how you dealt with it.
   Last year I was feeling pretty crummy all of the time. I was really worn out and just wanted to crash at home. Finally, I went to the Doctor and found out I had mono, which you get when you are really run down. It was no fun. I had to hang around and chill for a month, and had to take a lot of vitamins and couldn't eat any junk food or go out drinking. The worst part was that I flunked out and had to repeat the semester.
3. Which public figure do you admire and why?
   I really admire Bono because he is a cool guy. Instead of living the easy life and just partying and blowing his money, he does all these good works and helps unfortunate people and countries. He could just do his thing and people would appreciate him for his talent, but he is really into helping others and making the world a better place.
4. What is the hardest part of being a student?
   I'd say the biggest drag is having to concentrate on studying sometimes when you really don't feel like it. Like when you just want to lie around and do nothing, or go out and party, but you know there is a test and you'd better get to it or you'll never pull through. That is a real downer.

Corrigé

1. What do you like about being a student?

   It's cool being a student because you can learn a lot of interesting stuff and do fun things in your free time, like sports and stuff like that. You can find ways to travel and meet new buddies. Sometimes you get stressed out, like about grades and stuff like that, but most of the time it's pretty fun.

   It's really nice being a student because you are able to learn a lot of interesting things and do fun things in your free time, like sports and other activities. There are opportunities to travel and meet new people. Sometimes things can get stressful, like when it comes to grades and such, but most of the time it is really enjoyable.

2. Talk about a difficulty you encountered in the past year and how you dealt with it.

   Last year, I was feeling pretty crummy all of the time. I was really worn out and just wanted to crash at home. Finally I went to the Doctor and found out I had mono, which you get when you are really run down. It was no fun. I had to hang around and chill for a month, and had to take a lot of vitamins and couldn't eat any junk food or go out drinking. The worst part was that I flunked out and had to repeat the semester.

   Last year I was feeling under the weather all of the time. I was really tired and just wanted to stay home and relax. Finally, I went to the Doctor and found out I had mono, which you get when you are really worn down. It was no fun. I had to relax and take it easy for a month and had to take a lot of vitamins and avoid junk food and alcohol. The worst part was that I didn't pass my courses and I had to repeat the semester.

3. Which public figure do you admire and why?

   I think Bono is a cool guy. Instead of living the easy life and just partying and blowing his money, he does all these good works and helps unfortunate people and countries. He could just do his thing and people would appreciate him for his talent, but he is really into helping others and making the world a better place.

   In my opinion Bono is a really admirable person. Instead of just enjoying himself and his wealth, he is working on making the world a better place for those less fortunate. He could just rest on his laurels and people would appreciate him for his talent, but he is really dedicated to helping others and making the world a better place.

4. What is the hardest part of being a student?
   I'd say the biggest drag is having to concentrate on studying sometimes when you really don't feel like it. Like when you just want to lie around and do nothing, or go out and party, but you know there is a test and you'd better get to it or you'll never pull through. That is a real downer.
   I'd say the most difficult thing is having to concentrate on studying sometimes when you really don't feel like it. For example, when you just want to relax and do nothing, or go out and enjoy yourself, but you know there is a test and you'd better focus or you'll never pass. That is a real challenge.

CHAPITRE 7

Préparez-vous à la Writing Section

1. Les règles de base
2. La première rédaction, Integrated Writing
3. La deuxième rédaction, Independent Writing
4. Mise en application

Cette section du TOEFL iBT consiste en deux rédactions à faire en 50 minutes en tout.

Vous devrez rédiger la première, Integrated Writing, en 20 minutes. Vous aurez trois minutes pour lire un texte de 230 à 300 mots, ensuite deux minutes pour écouter un texte lu de la même longueur, ensuite quinze minutes pour rédiger tout en ayant le premier texte sous les yeux. Dans cette rédaction, il vous faudra comparer ou mettre en opposition les idées trouvées dans les deux textes. Cela veut dire qu'il faut être rapide, et même très rapide.

Dans la deuxième rédaction, Independent Writing, vous aurez 30 minutes pour prendre position et argumenter sur un sujet polémique. Ce travail peut sembler plus « classique » et donc plus facile. Rappelez-vous quand même que les auteurs du TOEFL iBT vous demandent un minimum de 300 mots et donc, qu'il faut pouvoir rédiger relativement vite.

1. Les règles de base

Voici une check-list des règles de base pour mettre toutes les chances de votre côté pour ces rédactions.

CHECK-LIST DES RÈGLES DE BASE	
a. Connaissez le clavier QWERTY.	Les auteurs du TOEFL iBT ont spécifié en clair que savoir écrire avec un clavier QWERTY est obligatoire.
b. Choisissez votre stratégie à l'avance.	Pour la rédaction Integrated Writing, donnez plus d'importance au texte lu à haute voix. Pour la rédaction Independent Writing, construisez un modèle de rédaction.
c. Evitez les formes contractées.	Les formes contractées font partie de la langue parlée.
d. Employez des structures et du vocabulaire que vous connaissez.	Même si votre choix de vocabulaire est rudimentaire, il vaut mieux rester maître de vos idées.
e. L'orthographe et la ponctuation : la petite bête.	Les erreurs d'orthographe ou de ponctuation ne sont graves que lorsqu'elles nuisent à la lisibilité du texte.

a. Connaissez le clavier QWERTY

Ce point n'est pas à négliger : tout candidat passe l'épreuve sur un clavier QWERTY. La tâche n'est pas facile pour un Français qui n'en a pas l'habitude. Cependant, comme l'ont voulu les concepteurs du TOEFL iBT, tous les candidats sont tenus de manier ce clavier avec facilité.

Voici comment se présente ce clavier :

Bien sûr, vous pouvez vous demander ce qui se passerait si vous décidiez d'« improviser », c'est-à-dire de pianoter tant bien que mal vos rédactions le jour J de l'examen.

D'abord, s'il y a trop d'erreurs de frappe, le correcteur comprendra probablement le message de votre texte, mais il comprendra aussi que vous n'êtes pas fonctionnel au clavier, et que vous n'avez pas respecté les consignes de l'examen. Rappelez-vous que le but du TOEFL iBT est de donner la preuve de votre adaptabilité aux universités américaines.

Ensuite, avec le temps limité, vous n'aurez pas le temps de recopier un texte rédigé au brouillon. Avec 30 minutes pour organiser ses idées et pour rédiger un minimum de 300 mots, il est clair que vous serez obligé de rédiger directement sur le clavier. Et le temps est trop court pour vous permettre de pianoter.

Il est recommandé de vous familiariser avec ce clavier avant l'épreuve. Vous pouvez coller des pastilles sur les lettres du clavier et le programmer pour le convertir en QWERTY. Tous les moyens sont bons : il faut devenir opérationnel sur un clavier QWERTY.

b. Choisissez votre stratégie à l'avance

Même si dans l'exercice de la partie Integrated Writing il s'agit de mettre en opposition (ou comparer) deux textes, la clé du succès réside dans une forte aptitude à la compréhension auditive.

Il faut d'abord lire le passage écrit pour en extraire l'idée générale et pour trouver une ou deux idées, si c'est possible. Prendre des notes est entièrement facultatif.

Ensuite, il faut écouter le texte lu en prenant des notes.

La dernière étape est d'utiliser ces notes comme référence de base pour votre rédaction faite directement au clavier, en rajoutant des idées du texte écrit que vous aurez encore sous les yeux.

Quant à la partie Independent Writing, les correcteurs du TOEFL iBT chercheront des formats de rédaction très précis pour répondre à un sujet précis (prise de position vis-à-vis d'une polémique).

Autant en profiter pour rédiger sa trame calmement chez soi. En préparant sa trame à l'avance, un candidat a forcément plus de temps pour rédiger sa réponse d'au moins 300 mots.

c. Evitez les formes contractées

Quelques minutes de lecture d'une revue ou d'un journal américain vous révéleront qu'aucune forme contractée ne figure dans la langue écrite (à part des citations de langue parlée) et ce serait une erreur fondamentale d'appréciation quant au style attendu dans cet examen que d'utiliser des formes contractées. Eviter également le style de type « chat » ou forum comme l'expression i. m. h. o. (in my humble opinion). Vous risqueriez d'agacer le correcteur.

d. Employez des structures et du vocabulaire que vous connaissez

Certains candidats peuvent se laisser entraîner à utiliser des mots de vocabulaire ou des expressions qu'ils ne connaissent pas. Notamment dans la partie Integrated Writing, où les auteurs du TOEFL iBT peuvent vous évaluer sur un texte où figurent des mots difficiles. Reprendre des mots dont vous ne connaissez pas le sens exact est une grosse erreur. En principe, vous vous êtes préparé pendant un certain temps pour cet examen et théoriquement votre vocabulaire est déjà assez riche pour vous permettre de vous exprimer convenablement. Il vaut mieux montrer ce que vous savez que de vous tromper sur ce que vous ne savez pas.

e. L'orthographe et la ponctuation : la petite bête

Combien de candidats, pendant un moment de doute, hésitent entre deux façons d'épeler un mot ? Dans un souci de bien faire, ils peuvent passer du temps précieux à se décider. Dans le contexte du TOEFL iBT, accorder beaucoup de temps à l'orthographe ou à la ponctuation, c'est chercher la petite bête.

Avec une limite de 15 minutes de rédaction en Integrated Writing et 30 minutes en Independent Writing, il est clair que le mot d'ordre est **clarté d'expression**. Si l'orthographe ou la ponctuation n'empêchent pas la lisibilité de la rédaction (ne pas employer de langage texto tout de même), alors ces fautes n'ont strictement aucune importance.

2. La première rédaction, Integrated Writing

Le but de cet exercice est de vérifier votre capacité à rédiger de manière fonctionnelle en tant qu'étudiant qui assiste à des conférences et fait ses devoirs, et qui a besoin de passer des examens ou de rédiger des rapports. Cet exercice évalue donc la capacité de combiner les fonctions auditive, de lecture, et rédactionnelle.

Le mot d'ordre pour cette partie de l'examen est « rapidité » : 3 minutes pour lire un texte, 2 minutes pour en écouter un autre, et 20 minutes en tout pour compléter la rédaction avec seulement le premier texte sous les yeux. Dans ces conditions, on n'a franchement pas le temps de s'attarder sur des mots ou des expressions.

Bien évidemment, l'entraînement à la compréhension auditive et à la lecture est très important pour réussir. Néanmoins, une stratégie de démarche devrait être adoptée dès maintenant.

1. *La clé du succès : l'écoute*

Quelques indices permettent de comprendre le rôle principal du texte lu dans la partie Integrated Writing.

En passant l'examen « Practice Online » du site www.toefl.org, on observe que la note obtenue, attribuée par eRater ®, un logiciel correcteur, est accompagnée d'une liste des critères de correction : il s'agit d'une liste des idées qui devaient impérativement figurer dans la rédaction. Bref, les attentes des correcteurs du TOEFL iBT sont précises et éliminatoires.

Que le candidat sache écrire des phrases en anglais en style élaboré ou pas, s'il n'inscrit pas les idées recherchées par le correcteur, sa note sera en dessous de 3.

Cette constatation se précise sur le tableau de critères des concepteurs du TOEFL iBT. Le descriptif de la note 3 est le suivant : « La réponse peut omettre une idée clé exprimée dans le texte écouté ».

Les notes supérieures sont aussi définies par rapport aux idées contenues dans la rédaction du candidat, surtout en fonction du texte écouté.

Rappelez-vous que vous aurez 3 minutes pour lire le premier texte et ensuite 15 minutes pour le consulter, si c'est nécessaire. Le passage de lecture est donc très accessible. En revanche, vous n'entendrez le texte lu qu'une seule fois pendant 2 minutes. Conclusion : la note se joue sur les idées qu'on peut tirer du texte écouté.

2. *Entraînement spécifique : les bêtes noires des étudiants français*

Puisque la compréhension auditive est si importante pour réussir la section Integrated Writing, nous vous présentons un entraînement spécifique, conçu spécialement pour les étudiants français.

Nous avons en effet observé, dans la salle de cours tous les jours, que trois points linguistiques sont particulièrement difficiles pour les étudiants français :

- les « phrasal verbs », qui n'existent pas en français, sont surtout enseignés à l'école à travers des exercices écrits et rarement à l'oral ;
- l'accent américain, n'est pas un point linguistique en soi, mais le matériel pédagogique en France s'appuie le plus souvent sur des accents anglais ;
- les « faux amis », souvent, eux aussi, plus souvent enseignés à l'écrit plutôt qu'à l'oral.

1. Phrasal verbs

Il s'agit de ces petites prépositions qui changent le sens du verbe d'origine et que tous ont vues au cours de leur scolarité.

Voici un exemple de phrasal verb :

He put his finger on the diary.	Il a posé son doigt sur l'agenda.
I won't put up with your lies.	Je ne vais pas tolérer tes mensonges.

Dans la première phrase, le verbe « put » veut dire « poser, mettre », mais dans la deuxième, grâce aux prépositions « up with », le phrasal verb « to put up with » veut dire « tolérer ».

Sans aucun doute, chacun a fait de nombreux exercices à l'écrit sur ce point de grammaire. Mais dans le contexte du TOEFL iBT, savoir remplir un blanc ne suffit pas. Il faut avoir assimilé la structure du phrasal verb dans la langue courante, notamment à la compréhension auditive.

Rappelez-vous que le texte entendu ne passera qu'une fois.

Writing Section, EXERCICE 1, Phrasal verbs

Consigne : écoutez le CD-ROM et choisissez la traduction correcte des phrases.

1. a. Au cas où il y aurait un peu de confusion sur la théorie de Leonardo Da Vinci, analysons-la.
   b. Au cas où il y aurait un peu de confusion sur la théorie de Leonardo Da Vinci, critiquons-la.

2. a. La raison pour laquelle on n'a pas pu réaliser cette expérience scientifique n'est pas compliquée. Cela revient à un manque de fonds.
   b. La raison pour laquelle on n'a pas pu réaliser cette expérience scientifique n'est pas compliquée ; ça a vraiment bouilli et n'a pas pu fondre.

3. a. En tant qu'inventeur du premier vaccin contre la polio, Jonas Salk a interrompu une série importante d'échecs.
   b. En tant qu'inventeur du premier vaccin contre la polio, Jonas Salk a fait une découverte importante.

4. a. Professor Wood a apporté son rapport qu'on attendait juste avant les vacances de Pâques.
   b. Professor Wood a évoqué le rapport à rendre juste avant les vacances de Pâques.

5. a. Un étudiant sérieux utilise toujours le surligneur pour les idées importantes qu'il parcourt dans ses lectures.
   b. Un étudiant sérieux résume toujours les idées importantes qu'il arrive à comprendre dans ses lectures.

6. a. A la fin de la conférence du Professeur Le Page sur l'élasticité, il y a eu de nombreuses questions les unes à la suite des autres.
   b. A la fin de la conférence du Professeur Le Page sur l'élasticité, il y a eu de nombreuses questions à propos de ses remarques.

7. a. Aucun étudiant en anthropologie ne veut faire trop de recherches.
   b. Aucun étudiant en anthropologie ne veut refaire ses recherches.

8. a. Est-ce que tout le groupe a calculé la réponse 128 000 ?
   b. Est-ce que tout le groupe a compris pourquoi la réponse est de 128 000 ?

9. a. Bien qu'il soit bien marqué sur le programme, Dr. Brown continuait à remettre le contrôle à plus tard.
   b. Bien qu'il soit bien marqué sur le programme, Dr. Brown continuait à annuler l'évaluation.

10. a. On va finir le cours d'aujourd'hui avec des diapos sur la période néandertalienne.
    b. On va discuter pendant le cours d'aujourd'hui des diapos sur la période néandertalienne.

11. a. Renseignez-vous sur la réservation du rétroprojecteur auprès de Mme Marciniak, la bibliothécaire.
    b. Regardez votre réservation du rétroprojecteur chez Mme Marciniak, la bibliothécaire.

12. a. Bien qu'Ernest Hemingway ne fût pas encore auteur confirmé lorsqu'il a commencé à habiter Paris, il avait déjà limité les choix du style qu'il adopterait plus tard dans ses ouvrages.
    b. Bien qu'Ernest Hemingway ne fût pas encore auteur confirmé lorsqu'il a commencé à habiter Paris, il avait déjà la possibilité d'utiliser le style journalistique qu'il adopterait plus tard dans ses ouvrages.

13. a. Je pourrais entamer le sujet de George Washington Carver, mais c'est la fin de ce cours.
    b. Je pourrais continuer à parler longuement de George Washington Carver, mais c'est la fin de ce cours.

14. a. La semaine dernière, nous nous sommes quittés avant de parler d'Attila et les Huns et leurs voyages partout en Europe.
    b. La semaine dernière, nous en sommes restés sur le sujet d'Attila et les Huns et leurs voyages partout en Europe.

15. a. Le contrôle d'aujourd'hui sera distribué dans la semaine.
    b. Le contrôle d'aujourd'hui sera rendu la semaine prochaine.

2. L'accent américain

Rappelez-vous que le TOEFL iBT est un examen américain. Mis à part un texte qui peut être lu par un narrateur anglophone (anglais, écossais, irlandais, etc.), tous les autres textes seront lus avec des accents américains. L'adaptation n'est pas facile pour un étudiant qui a l'habitude d'entendre l'accent britannique (ou français) en cours. Pourtant, il faut absolument s'y faire.

Writing Section, EXERCICE 2, L'accent américain

Consigne : écoutez le CD-rom et choisissez la traduction correcte des phrases.

1. a. Avez-vous payé votre loyer pour le mois d'avril ?
   b. Avez-vous vu les parents au mois d'avril ?

2. a. Ma facture eau-gaz-électricité est excessive.
   b. L'aide de Bill est providentielle.

3. a. Est-ce que les chiens n'ont pas trop chaud ?
   b. Est-ce qu'on peut acheter des hot dogs ?

4. a. Qu'est-ce qu'il y a ? Tu n'as pas encore écrit la note interne ?
   b. Qu'est-ce qu'il y a ? Tu n'as pas encore trouvé un stage ?

5. a. Voulez-vous encore du beurre ?
   b. Vous en voulez encore meilleur ?

6. a. Envoyez votre résumé de texte le plus rapidement possible.
   b. Veuillez envoyer votre CV le plus rapidement possible.

7. a. Que pensez-vous de l'homme de l'Arkansas ?
   b. Que pensez-vous de l'homme que j'ai vu ?

8. a. J'ai une indigestion.
   b. Je dois faire le plein.

9. a. Qu'est-ce qu'il avait fait pour mériter cela ?
   b. Qu'est-ce qu'il a fait pour mériter cela ?

10. a. Allez-vous tous ensemble vous raser la barbe ?
    b. Allez-vous au centre commercial avec Barbara ?

3. Les « faux amis »

Dès les premiers cours d'anglais, on parle de « faux amis », ces mots vicieux qui ressemblent en orthographe à des mots français mais qui n'ont pas le même sens en anglais. La mauvaise compréhension d'un seul « faux ami » peut causer des contresens de textes entiers.

Il est clair que la plupart des candidats reconnaissent beaucoup de « faux amis » à la lecture. Pour la section Integrated Writing, il va falloir les reconnaître à l'écoute, et rapidement. Vous n'aurez pas le temps de les traduire ; il faudra les avoir assimilés.

Writing Section, EXERCICE 3, Les « faux amis »

Consigne : écoutez le CD-rom et choisissez la traduction correcte des phrases.

1. a. En ce moment, les tremblements de terre ont lieu tous les jours.
   b. En réalité, des tremblements de terre ont lieu tous les jours.
2. a. Hier soir, George a été présent au spectacle de magie.
   b. Hier soir, George a donné un coup de main au spectacle de magie.
3. a. Mike a réussi son bac.
   b. Mike est un célibataire confirmé.
4. a. Il y aura un retard de 20 minutes.
   b. Il y aura une période de 20 minutes.
5. a. Jayne a rendu son examen.
   b. Jayne a réussi son examen.
6. a. Ils se sont rendu compte que l'étude de marché était précise.
   b. Ils ont effectué une étude de marché précise.
7. a. Jack est le garçon le plus émotif que j'ai jamais connu.
   b. Jack est le garçon le plus sensé que j'ai jamais connu.
8. a. Son grand-père est un type sympa.
   b. Son grand-père est du genre compréhensif.
9. a. Mathew était en formation la semaine dernière.
   b. Mathew était en scène la semaine dernière.
10. a. Gone with the wind, by Margaret Mitchell, est en librairie.
    b. Gone with the wind, by Margaret Mitchell, est à la bibliothèque.

(Corrections au chapitre 10)

Si vous avez fait beaucoup de fautes aux trois derniers exercices, il faut impérativement revoir ces points linguistiques. Ne pas se contenter de connaître de manière passive les phrasal verbs, l'accent américain, et les « faux amis », mais les maîtriser réellement est essentiel pour la section Integrated Writing du TOEFL iBT.

4. La méthode pour réussir la section Integrated Writing

Pour réussir à décrocher une bonne note à la section Integrated Writing, les trois premières minutes de lecture devraient servir à trouver le sujet du texte et à déceler une ou deux idées contenues dans le texte. Cette lecture devrait vous orienter vers une écoute efficace dans la mesure où vous pouvez déjà anticiper le sujet. Ensuite, écoutez le texte lu en prenant des notes dans le but de dégager un maximum d'idées. Une fois l'enregistrement terminé, développez vos notes : ce sera le squelette de votre rédaction. La dernière étape est de rajouter des idées **du passage** du texte écrit que vous aurez sous les yeux.

L'exemple suivant illustre la façon de procéder avec le texte entendu. Supposons que vous venez de lire un texte écrit dont le sujet est : « Rare court cases in the UK in 1998 ». Maintenant, écoutez le CD-rom et prenez des notes :

Writing Section, EXERCICE 4, Résumé de texte 1

Consigne : écoutez le CD-ROM et prenez des notes.

Voici un exemple des notes que vous auriez pu prendre :

Notes :

Kids take parents to court/accidents/horrible idea : reputation/name used for legal papers/settled out of court/fault of lawyers/breaking down families

Maintenant, c'est à vous de rédiger à partir de ces notes tout de suite après avoir écouté le texte. Si vous préférez, vous pouvez rédiger des phrases qui correspondent aux idées principales. Par exemple :

1. A law firm encouraged children to bring their parents to court in the UK in 1998, but was condemned.
2. Parents do not need to go to court, and children sue the parents' insurance company : reputations are untouched.
3. That law firm only wanted to make more money by breaking down the family unit.

A partir de ces phrases, ou directement au clavier et à l'écran après l'écoute, la prochaine étape est de résumer le texte écouté. Voici un exemple de résumé du texte entendu de cet exercice :

The lecture deals with insurance claims made by children against their parents. In 1998, in the UK, a law firm which encouraged children to sue parents for injuries happening at home, was widely condemned. Their idea was that companies would definitely pay and that parents would make money through their children without risking their reputation, since most of these cases are settled out of court. However, the Federation of Insurance Lawyers felt such tactics would break families down, just make lawyers richer and force parents to pay higher premiums in the long run.

Maintenant que le résumé du texte écouté est rédigé, les idées contraires ou similaires peuvent être rajoutées au fur et à mesure à l'écran. Ces rajouts seront précédés des mots de vocabulaire de contraste ou de comparaison que vous trouverez dans la liste au chapitre **8**. A titre d'exemple,

« whereas the passage indicates that... »
« This directly contradicts what the standpoint of the reading. »
« However, the passage claims that... »
« ... contrary to what the reading passage says. »

sont des transitions possibles pour rajouter les idées principales du passage du texte écrit à votre résumé du texte écouté.

La méthode est donc la suivante : lecture du texte écrit, écoute du passage oral, résumé du passage écouté, rajouts d'idées du texte écrit.

Voici quelques exercices vous permettant de vous entraîner pour la section Integrated Writing : un résumé du texte entendu et un relevé des idées opposées dans les deux textes.

Writing Section, EXERCICE 5, Résumé de texte 2

Consigne : écoutez le CD-ROM et prenez des notes. Ensuite, rédigez un résumé de texte. Consultez la clé au chapitre **10**.

Writing Section, EXERCICE 6, Relevé des idées opposées dans les deux textes

Consigne : lisez le texte suivant pendant 3 minutes. Ensuite, écoutez le texte lu à haute voix sur le CD-ROM. Trouvez les idées opposées dans les deux textes, et consultez la clé au chapitre 10.

Arnold Schoenberg was born in Austria in 1874 and later became an American citizen. This composer is most especially remembered as the founder of atonality or the twelve-tone technique. In the 1500's, music was written in modal organization, followed by the major-minor key system, established in the late 1600's. All of this music, continuing up until 1900, is based on a system of tonal hierarchies or arranged around tonal centers. When Schoenberg and others began composing music in the twelve-tone technique, they insisted that the major-minor key system had been exhausted over the years and that « one tonal chord could not assert dominance over all of the others ». Thanks to Schoenberg, musical atonality was born.

Schoenberg is well-known because his was the first attempt to avoid traditional diatonic harmony and was, in turn, the beginning of a modern movement in music. This movement was to continue, as Pierre Boulez, Milton Babbitt, Elliott Carter, and Igor Stravinsky composed with the twelve-tone scale. Atonal music continues to be composed today, and Schoenberg is the father of these compositions.

One of Schoenberg's important works is Pierrot Lunaire, a series of songs set to a text by Albert Giraud. It is sung by a female singer dressed in a Pierrot costume with a group of 5 musicians, who play musical instruments. Pierrot Lunaire is recognized around the world as a keystone musical composition.

In conclusion, it is obvious that Arnold Schoenberg, with his atonal concept, is an influential composer of modern times.

3. La deuxième rédaction, Independent Writing

Contrairement à l'épreuve précédente, la rédaction Independent Writing est une réponse à une question écrite, qui présente une polémique. Il n'y a aucun texte à écouter. Le candidat doit dégager les idées exprimées dans le sujet, prendre position par rapport à ces idées, développer sa position, et conclure. Il faudra donc argumenter, car le but de l'exercice est la rédaction d'un texte convaincant et élaboré.

Cet exercice est simple en soi, mais il présente un obstacle majeur : il faut pouvoir produire 300 mots « ou plus » en 30 minutes. Soyons clairs : si les concepteurs du TOEFL iBT précisent « ou plus », nous pouvons comprendre qu'une bonne note n'est donnée qu'à une rédaction d'un strict minimum de 300 mots. Bien sûr, nous soulignons de nouveau l'importance d'une maîtrise totale du clavier QWERTY, ainsi que de la capacité à manier les structures nécessaires de l'anglais américain. Pour pouvoir produire une rédaction d'une telle ampleur en si peu de temps, il est clair que les candidats bien préparés auront un gros avantage sur les autres.

1. L'introduction

Le fond

Qui n'a pas appris à l'école que l'introduction est un élément clé d'une rédaction ? Tout ce que vous avez appris sur l'importance de l'introduction reste valable pour la rédaction Independent Writing du TOEFL iBT. Parlons donc de ce qui est différent.

Tout d'abord, il faut noter la nature du sujet. Ce sujet portera sur une polémique, et donc, il y aura forcément au moins deux points de vue à exposer. Exposer un point de vue, le vôtre, ne suffit pas.

Ensuite, l'entrée en matière dans une rédaction à l'anglo-saxonne est toujours rapide. Le candidat est tenu d'annoncer sa position dès le premier paragraphe. Une longue introduction sans prise de position sera inévitablement mal perçue par un correcteur.

Voici un exemple d'un sujet suivi de quelques introductions types que nous commenterons :

> Do you agree or disagree with the following statement?
> Every human being should have the right to terminate or to ask another to terminate his life.
> Use reasons and specific details to support your answer.

Introduction 1

Some people believe euthanasia is right. Some people don't. Indeed, the right to terminate life is a tough question.

Introduction 2

It is true that euthanasia is wrong, according to certain religions. Death should be the decision of God and not of men. All Christians would like to see euthanasia against the law. I agree with the contention that euthanasia should be banned.

Introduction 3

The issue of euthanasia, due to the responsibilities it puts on doctors and family members, is a controversial one. On the one hand, a ban on euthanasia is a direct infringement on a sick person's liberty to put an end to his horrible suffering. On the other hand, judges or doctors should not be obliged to overtly kill their fellow man. However, in the final analysis, I believe that terminating one's life is a personal choice that should be granted to every human being.

Introduction 4

The traditional stance that euthanasia is against religion and against the law of God has become increasingly challenged in today's world. Fewer people are strictly religious nowadays, and many interpret religious precepts in their own way. Moreover, modern developments in the medical field have created many more situations in which a patient's life can be prolonged for years with no improvement, leaving the patient and his family in a state of limbo. This essay will discuss different aspects of euthanasia, past and present, and why, for me, a taboo is gradually lifting.

Si ces quatre introductions étaient soumises au TOEFL iBT aujourd'hui, elles seraient notées différemment.

La première, trop courte, ne fait que reformuler la question. Sa conclusion, « the right to terminate life is a tough question », ne rajoute strictement rien à la polémique et ne dévoile pas du tout la position de l'auteur sur l'euthanasie. La rédaction qui suit sera peut-être excellente, mais la première impression donnée à travers l'introduction, mérite un petit point et pas plus.

La deuxième introduction est plus longue. Elle évoque l'argument religieux pour défendre sa position contre l'euthanasie. Surtout, le candidat exprime son avis dans cette introduction sans attendre le deuxième paragraphe. Pour son élaboration et sa prise de position, cette introduction obtiendrait la note de 2-3 points. Et pourquoi pas 4-5 points ? Tout simplement parce qu'elle n'a présenté qu'un aspect de la polémique. Elle ne tient pas compte de l'opinion de ceux qui soutiennent l'euthanasie, et pour cette raison, elle n'est pas complète.

La troisième introduction, plus longue encore, répond aux deux critères. Elle tient compte des deux aspects de la polémique avec un premier élément d'analyse : la souffrance des malades, la responsabilité des médecins. Après sa constatation de la situation, le candidat prend position. De toutes les trois, cette introduction est la plus élaborée et obtiendrait la note de 4-5 points.

La quatrième introduction est aussi élaborée que la troisième, mais un peu différente. Elle présente deux aspects de la polémique, mais cette fois-ci, l'analyse n'est pas la même : elle met en opposition les croyances religieuses d'autrefois et les nouvelles situations créées par les avances scientifiques en médecine. Le candidat présente donc deux aspects de la polémique (l'ancien/le moderne), en décrivant une évolution dans les points de vue populaires vis-à-vis de l'euthanasie. Après sa constatation de la situation, ce candidat prend aussi position, mais de manière plus subtile. En utilisant le mot « taboo », le candidat sous-entend qu'il est en faveur de l'euthanasie, et qu'il pense que les « tabous religieux » disparaîtront un jour. Comme la troisième, cette dernière introduction obtiendrait 4-5 points.

La forme

Puisque les auteurs du TOEFL iBT ont annoncé d'avance que la rédaction Independent Writing sera une réponse à la présentation d'une polémique, il est possible de préparer sa trame personnelle à l'avance. Au chapitre **8**, vous trouverez le vocabulaire nécessaire pour vous aider à construire la trame qui vous convient.

Voici quelques trames d'introduction qui répondent au sujet proposé en Independent Writing :

Trame 1

The issue of ______________________ due to ______________________ is controversial. On the one hand, ______________________. On the other hand, ______________________. However, in the long run, I believe that ______________________

Trame 2

The problem of ______________________________ is difficult to deal with due to _______________. Many people think that __________________ because ____________________. On the contrary, __________________ can also be partly justified because ____________________. In my opinion, the fact remains that _______________.

Trame 3

The issue of ________________________ may be considered in different ways because of ______ ______________. It is often believed that ________________. However, it is also true that __________________. Taking all aspects into account, I strongly feel that ______________.

Le corps de la rédaction

Le fond : la recherche d'idées

Qu'elle ait lieu avant ou après la rédaction de l'introduction, la recherche rapide d'idées, ou « brainstorming » en anglais, est une étape nécessaire. Cette recherche sert à dégager un maximum d'idées pour mieux argumenter lors de la rédaction. Elle est donc nécessaire, mais plus elle est organisée et faite avec un objectif précis, plus elle sera utile à la rédaction.

Voici un exemple qui permettra d'expérimenter une méthode de travail :

> Some teenagers have jobs while they are still students. Others concentrate on their studies and enter the working world when they have finished their degree. Which of these two situations do you prefer ? Give reasons and specific details.

Pour le travail	Contre le travail
Expérience dans la vie active	Réussite à l'école
Ouverture vers l'avenir	Peut-être une ouverture vers d'autres diplômes
Savoir parler avec des clients, un patron	
Confiance en soi, maturité	
Argent de poche	

Même si le candidat qui a fait cette recherche d'idées est étudiant à plein-temps et heureux de sa situation, est-ce qu'il a vraiment intérêt à défendre une position contre le travail ? Comme il a noté cinq idées dans la colonne « pour », sa rédaction de 300 mots sera beaucoup plus riche s'il défend le travail en même temps que les études.

L'objectif précis de votre recherche d'idées devrait être donc de déterminer la position que vous allez défendre dans votre rédaction. C'est une démarche pragmatique de choisir « votre » opinion selon le nombre d'idées trouvées pour la défendre : exprimer un avis au TOEFL iBT devrait être un choix stratégique et non pas un choix personnel.

La forme : recommandations rédactionnelles

Référez-vous au chapitre **8**, pour voir la liste de vocabulaire qui vous aidera à construire une trame personnelle. Voici quelques idées de trame pour le corps de la rédaction :

Paragraphe 1

First, I agree/disagree with this statement because ____________________.

The first reason I believe this is ____________________.

One of the reasons for my belief is ____________________.

To begin with, it is true that ____________________.

Paragraphe 2

Second, ____________________.

The second reason for my opinion is ____________________.

Another way to justify my point of view is ____________________.

It is also widely accepted that ____________________.

Paragraphe 3

Third, ____________________.

Last but not least, I am firmly convinced that ____________________.

Most importantly, ____________________.

The biggest reason certainly is ____________________.

People also tend to think that ________________________________.

Ces phrases sont proposées à titre de renseignement, pour donner des idées de rédaction. Rien n'empêche de les personnaliser, ni de rajouter un quatrième paragraphe.

Des arguments directs et précis

Dans les cours de littérature américaine, on apprend toujours que le « style américain » de Fitzgerald ou d'Hemingway est direct et « journalistique ». Ce style est à adopter pour la rédaction Independent Writing. Plus les arguments sont directs et précis, plus la note augmentera. Si vos professeurs à l'école vous ont conseillé un style rédactionnel élaboré, voire « proustien », il vaut mieux ranger vos notes le jour du TOEFL iBT. Les phrases longues et compliquées sont à éviter.

Voici un exemple :

Do you agree or disagree with the following statement?
The study of History is a complete entity. Everything that has transpired and ever will transpire is already written in History books, since man constantly repeats his same acts and behaviors.
Use reasons and specific details to support your answer.

Une rédaction non concise

The first reason why I believe that it is fundamental to study History with its many dates, time perspectives, and unforgettable figures is that there are lessons to learn for young and old, day by day. Concentrating on the present and shunning past events with their behavioral twists and turns is deliberately turning one's back to the hundreds of humankind's psychological portraits in a vast gallery of art.

Une rédaction concise et précise

First, I agree with this statement because the study of History offers fundamental lessons to all, regardless of age. Concentrating on the present is useless if one does not remember these lessons of the past.

La deuxième rédaction est peut-être moins « littéraire » que la première, mais sa clarté sera bien appréciée par le correcteur du TOEFL iBT.

EXERCICE 7, Des arguments directs et précis

Consigne : récrivez les rédactions suivantes dans un style plus direct

1. The second explanation as to why I believe the study of History is throwing precious time out of the window is that most of the time, the tedious research to be conducted is just abundantly full of birth dates, death dates, useless biographies, and many uninteresting facts and figures concerning dead people who will never come back to life, anyway. How will the year Thomas Edison went to school further the progress of science, invent new music, and play the baseball, basketball, and football games of today with our living bodies and minds ?

2. As a last and final reason for which I wish to uphold a moderate study of History, not too much and not too little, I believe that certain facts can be beneficial and teach students necessary lessons which can change their perspective on their lives in the present. For instance, all young people from different countries, from childhood to teenage years, should be obliged, forced, and required to know the facts, figures, and events of World War II, the bombs, the criminal acts, and the atrocities which man inflicted upon his fellow man.

(Corrections au chapitre 10)

Des mots de structure

L'usage de mots de structure, parsemés partout dans votre rédaction, est primordial. Ces mots devraient se positionner dans des endroits clés, comme si l'on consultait une carte géographique, car leur rôle est l'orientation du lecteur. Certains mots, qui évoquent des exemples, qui indiquent le rajout d'une idée, qui soulignent l'importance d'une idée, qui indiquent une conclusion ou une contradiction, apparaissent comme des panneaux sur le bord de la route pour guider le lecteur.

EXERCICE 8, Des mots de structure

Consigne : choisissez le mot qui convient dans la phrase.

1. A number two pencil was compulsory for the computer-corrected exam that afternoon ; ____________________ Carol quickly drove to the nearest book store to buy a few.

   A. so
   B. besides
   C. also
   D. for instance

2. Weatherproofing enhances long-term wear for leather and suede boots; ________________, the majority of the boots on the market these days are of synthetic blend.
   A. consequently C. for example
   B. moreover D. nevertheless

3. It is statistically proven that 50 % of the population in the Midwest moves south; ________________ luggage is a good product to sell in this region.
   A. however C. nevertheless
   B. thus D. also

4. That dog hadn't seen his master for ages; ________________, at the end of the war, he recognized him right away, followed him home and showed respect for him for years to come.
   A. meanwhile C. however
   B. besides D. moreover

5. These new computers can improve our office efficiency; ________________, they can keep our costs down.
   A. however C. furthermore
   B. nevertheless D. nonetheless

6. Since the Puritans didn't want the British to know their identities, they held the Boston Tea Party very secretively; ________________, they wore Indian clothes to Boston Harbor.
   A. however C. on the whole
   B. moreover D. nonetheless

(Corrections au chapitre 10)

Pour toute lacune vis-à-vis de la signification des mots de structure, consultez le chapitre 8.

Maintenant, regardons un exemple de l'usage de mots de structure :

Some people believe that there could be life on another planet. Others believe that man is the only living creature in the universe. Which of these two positions do you agree with? Give reasons and specific details.

Une rédaction sans mots de structure

It is obvious that there is life somewhere in another galaxy. The universe is so vast that it would be hard to imagine the contrary. There is just no reason why human beings should be the only life to exist anywhere. It would not surprise me some day to hear NASA pick up a signal from other creatures, just as we sent out a message with the description of a man and a woman across the universe. Although we have not yet met, I believe that man's encounter with other life is an inevitable future event.

Une rédaction avec des mots de structure

<u>As far as I am concerned</u>, it is obvious that there is life somewhere in another galaxy. <u>On the one hand</u>, the universe is so vast that it would be hard to imagine the contrary. <u>On the other hand</u>, there is just no reason why human beings should be the only life to exist anywhere. <u>For instance</u>, it would not surprise me some day to hear NASA pick up a signal from other creatures, just as we sent out a message with the description of a man and a woman across the universe. <u>Therefore</u>, <u>in my opinion</u>, although we have not yet met, I believe that man's encounter with other life is an inevitable future event.

EXERCICE 9, Le rajout des mots de structure

Consigne : récrivez les paragraphes suivants en utilisant des mots de structure.

1. Knowing if there is life somewhere in outer space has been intriguing mankind for centuries. There is definitely life on other planets. Other beings will some day come to Earth to conquer our planet, and we humans will have to bow down to new leaders. We can see pictures of UFO's in the newspaper every day. I believe that our day of reckoning is yet to come.

2. There is no possible life on other planets. Man is God's uniquely created being, and there is no other planet in our solar system on which humans could survive. If there were life on another planet, wouldn't we know it by now? That is why man has to be the only creature in the universe.

(Corrections au chapitre 10)

L'illustration

L'illustration est un outil pratique pour plusieurs raisons. Tout d'abord, l'illustration fait partie des « specific details » ou détails précis mentionnés évoqués dans le sujet de rédaction. Ces détails sont nécessaires pour pouvoir développer vos arguments. De plus, l'illustration est un excellent moyen d'atteindre le minimum de 300 mots de rédaction au TOEFL iBT. Il faut illustrer pour remplir la page, de préférence, une illustration par paragraphe. Il ne faut surtout pas avoir peur de manquer d'expérience, car les observations ou la lecture sont aussi sources d'exemples.

Voici comment insérer une illustration :

Do you agree or disagree with the following statement?
Clothes make the man.
Use reasons and specific details to support your answer.

Avant l'insertion de l'illustration

First of all, although many people will deny it, the fact is that appearance is crucial in this day and age. As a matter of fact, it is a real challenge to go through the rituals of everyday life without adhering to a certain dress code imposed by our society. Just a mismatch of respective dress codes would most likely lead to scoffing and even rejection by other community members.

Après l'insertion de l'illustration

First of all, although many people will deny it, the fact is that appearance is crucial in this day and age. As a matter of fact, can anyone imagine the CEO of a well-known company showing up to work with sweatpants and sneakers, rather than the three-piece suit imposed on him by society? Such a mismatch of respective dress codes would most likely lead to scoffing and even rejection by other company members.

Les exemples peuvent être longs ou courts ; l'essentiel est qu'il en figure dans votre texte. Un correcteur qui constate une rédaction sans illustration va forcément la pénaliser.

La conclusion

Le fond

La conclusion (dernier paragraphe) reformule le point de vue exprimé sur le sujet sans reprendre les arguments des paragraphes précédents. Elle est courte, claire, et clôture la discussion. Surtout, elle ne comporte pas de nouvelles idées.

Certes, une conclusion élaborée est peut-être convaincante, mais pas prioritaire. S'il ne reste pas beaucoup de temps à la fin de l'épreuve, il vaut mieux la rédiger rapidement pour pouvoir passer les dernières minutes à se relire pour corriger les fautes de structure.

La forme

Consultez le chapitre 8 pour la liste de vocabulaire qui vous aidera à construire une trame personnelle. Voici quelques idées de trame pour la conclusion :

In conclusion, my firm belief is that ______________________________

For all these reasons, I think that ______________________________

In the final analysis, I agree/disagree with ______________________________

To sum up, I feel that ______________________________

In short, my strong conviction is that ______________________________

In a nutshell, I would say that ______________________________

In summary, my stance on this issue is ______________________________

4. Mise en application

EXERCICE 10 : Maintenant, c'est à vous de mettre en application tout ce que vous venez de lire dans ce chapitre. Faites une rédaction à partir du plan suivant. Vous trouverez un « corrigé » dans la clé au chapitre 10.

Question :

Do you agree or disagree with the following statement ?
Never mix business with pleasure.
Use reasons and specific details to support your answer

1. Introduction : my opinion, they do not mix
   Business : companies and the rules of business
   Pleasure : relaxation and fun
2. Second paragraph : pleasure mixes with business
   Survival of business which determines the amount of pleasure allowed
   Mixture only to a certain extent
3. Third paragraph : pleasure and business mix every day
   Such mixtures remain details
   Reason : risk of loss of business
4. Fourth paragraph : business mixed with pleasure
   Only for a short time
   Reason : can be too boring
5. Last paragraph : business and pleasure do not mix
   Reason : their respective natures
   Not fundamentally compatible

(Corrections au chapitre 10)

CHAPITRE 8

Maîtrisez parfaitement le vocabulaire essentiel pour réussir au TOEFL iBT

Vocabulaire de base – Reading Section

1. mandatory	Obligatoire
2. to postpone	Remettre à plus tard
3. nimble	Agile
4. a commitment	Un engagement
5. inept	Incompétent
6. to coerce	Forcer
7. a statement	Une affirmation
8. to be akin to	Ressembler à
9. a blunder	Une erreur
10. to depict	Caractériser
11. to enhance	Améliorer
12. to ensue	Suivre
13. flimsy	Léger, peu crédible
14. a limb	Un bras ou une jambe
15. to meddle in	Se mêler de
16. an ordeal	Une épreuve
17. prevalent	Dominant
18. remnants	Des restes
19. to surmise	Soupçonner
20. terse	Bref
21. to falter	Hésiter
22. a premise	Une hypothèse
23. sporadic	Irrégulier
24. forbearance	La patience
25. a grudge	Une rancune
26. to repel	Rejeter
27. turmoil	La confusion
28. output	La production
29. to advocate	Soutenir, préconiser
30. hardly	À peine
31. a flaw	Un défaut
32. to dwindle	Diminuer
33. to be doomed	Être condamné
34. to thrive	Prospérer, s'épanouir
35. minute	Minuscule
36. to impinge upon	Empiéter sur, affecter

Vocabulaire rédactionnel – Writing Section

Words used for comparisons	*Vocabulaire des comparaisons*
Alike, like	Semblable, comme
similar/similarities	Similaire/des similarités
Identical	Identique
Likewise	De même, aussi
Comparable to	Comparable à
By the same token	Pareillement
Words used for contrasts	***Vocabulaire des contrastes***
Unlike	Dissemblable
In contrast with	Par contraste avec
Whereas	Tandis que
Is different from/differs from	Est différent de/se différencie de
Conversely	Contrairement
More than/less than/fewer than	Plus que/moins de/moins que
On the contrary	Au contraire
First of all/to begin with	Tout d'abord/Pour commencer
First/Second/Third/Finally	En premier lieu, en deuxième lieu, enfin
Firstly/Secondly/Thirdly/Finally	Premièrement, deuxièmement, troisièmement, enfin
On the one hand...on the other hand	D'une part...d'autre part
For one thing...for another	D'une part...d'autre part
accurate/specific	Exact/précis
convincing/sound	Convaincant/solide
reasons/arguments	Des raisons/des arguments
To take into account/to consider	Prendre en compte/en considération
As a matter of fact	En fait
To face the facts	Regarder les choses en face
The fact remains that...	Il n'en est pas moins vrai que...
In this respect	A cet égard
In support of this statement	A l'appui de cette constatation
For example/for instance	Par exemple
To illustrate this point/my point	Pour illustrer ce que je veux dire
It is obvious/clear that...	Il est évident que...

By all rights	En principe
The steps/procedure for	Les étapes/la démarche pour
The advantages/disadvantages of	Les avantages/les inconvénients de
The pros/cons of	Les avantages/les inconvénients de
The ways to/the methods of	Le chemin vers/la méthode pour
The characteristics/traits/qualities of	Les caractéristiques de
The precautions for	Les précautions pour
The reasons for	Les raisons de
The causes/effects of	Les causes/effets de
different sections/parts/types/kinds	Différentes parties/sortes/différents genres
The problems of	Les problèmes de
The changes to	Les modifications à
Despite/In spite of	Malgré/en dépit de
Rather than	Plutôt que
Instead of	Au lieu de
Although	Bien que
Besides/moreover	D'ailleurs
Consequently/as a result	Par conséquent
Nevertheless	Néanmoins
On the whole	Dans l'ensemble
However/yet	Cependant
For this purpose	Dans ce but (pour cela)
Thus	Ainsi
Therefore	Donc
Furthermore/in addition	De plus
Meanwhile	Pendant ce temps
Surely/Clearly/Certainly	Certainement
Undoubtedly	Sans doute
Obviously,/Of course,/True,	Evidemment, bien sûr, il est vrai que
One cannot deny that	On ne peut pas nier que...
Granted,	Je vous l'accorde,

I tend to view this issue...	J'ai tendance à considérer cette polémique...
I agree/I disagree with	Je suis d'accord/je ne suis pas d'accord avec

Most people would agree that...	La plupart des gens seraient d'accord pour dire...
This conviction can be partly justified	Cette conviction peut se justifier en partie
I think people are wrong/are right...	Je pense que les gens ont tort/ont raison
There is every reason to believe that	Il y a tout lieu de croire que...
Nowadays/presently	De nos jours/actuellement
To claim	Prétendre
My opinion/point of view/conviction	Mon opinion/point de vue/conviction
Compelling	Attrayant
To support one's position	Soutenir son point de vue
Last but not least	Le dernier mais non le moindre
To conclude/In conclusion	Pour conclure/en conclusion
To sum up/In short	Pour résumer

In the final analysis	En fin de compte
In a nutshell	En deux mots, bref
In summary	Pour résumer

LE SYSTEME UNIVERSITAIRE AUX USA
THE U.S. UNIVERSITY SYSTEM

Cycle	Diplôme	Années d'étude	Nom de l'année
Undergraduate Studies	– BA Bachelor of Arts – BS Bachelor of Science	1st 2nd 3rd 4th	Freshman year Sophomore year Junior year Senior year
	– MA Master of Arts – MS Master of Science – MBA Master of Business Administration	1-2 years, plus Master's Thesis	
Graduate Studies	– PhD – Doctorate	1-2 years, plus Doctoral Thesis	

LE SYSTEME DE NOTATION AUX USA
U.S. GRADING SYSTEM

Il y a trois systèmes de notation :

Le système 4-0	Le système A-F	Le système de pourcentage 100-60 %	L'appréciation
4	A	100-90 %	Excellent (Excellent)
3	B	89-80 %	Good (Bien)
2	C	79-70 %	Satisfactory (Satisfaisant)
1	D	69-60 %	Barely Passing (Passable)
0	F	59 % et moins	Failure (Echec)

L'UNIVERSITE – UNIVERSITY

University terms	*Vocabulaire de l'université*
1. to drop out	Quitter l'université avant la fin des études
2. to work one's way through university	Travailler pour pouvoir payer ses études
3. campus	La faculté
4. a faculty	Le corps enseignant
5. a major	Une spécialisation
6. to major in a subject	Se spécialiser dans une matière
7. to graduate	Avoir son diplôme
8. graduate students	Des élèves dans la 5e année d'études
9. undergraduate students	Des élèves dans les premières quatre années de l'université
10. financial aid	Aide financière
11. a scholarship	Une bourse d'études
12. registration/enrollment	l'inscription
13. tuition	Les frais d'inscription
14. dormitory	Le dortoir

15. a term paper	Un rapport de fin de trimestre
16. a mid-term exam	Un partiel
17. a final exam	Un examen final
18. a lecture course	Un cours magistral
19. an alumnus	Un ancien élève
20. alumni	Les anciens élèves
21. an internship	Un stage
22. credits	Des unités de valeur
23. a pre-requisite	Un cours qu'un étudiant doit suivre pour pouvoir s'inscrire dans un autre cours
24. class curriculum	Le programme d'un cours
25. a teaching assistant	Un candidat au doctorat qui donne des cours
25. to ace an exam	Réussir un examen
26. admissions office	Bureau d'inscription
27. to pull an all-nighter	Réviser toute la nuit
28. to audit	Assister à un cours en candidat libre
29. to call the roll	Vérifier la présence
30. a carrel	Un petit espace pour réviser à la bibliothèque
31. coed	Pour hommes et pour femmes
32. a college	Une petite université
33. to cram	Réviser à la dernière minute
34. a curve	Un barème
35. to cut class/to skip class	Sécher un cours
36. a dean	Un doyen
37. a department chair	Le chef d'un département
38. a dorm/dormitory	Un dortoir
39. a draft	Un brouillon
40. fill-in-the-blank test/multiple-choice test	QCM
41. G.P.A./grade point average	La moyenne des notes (d'un étudiant)
42. a handout	Des cours préparés par un prof, distribués aux étudiants
43. a makeup test	Un examen de rattrapage
44. a quiz	Un petit contrôle

45. room and board	Les frais du dortoir et de la cantine
46. the stacks	Les rayons de livres à la bibliothèque
47. student union	Le bâtiment pour les affaires des étudiants
48. tenure	La titularisation
49. a transcript	Un record officiel de la scolarité et des notes
50. an advisor	Un conseiller universitaire
51. an assignment	Un devoir
52. to be behind	Être en retard dans son travail
53. to check out	Emprunter des livres ou d'autres supports de la bibliothèque
54. an elective	Un cours facultatif
55. honors	Avec mention
56. quarter : fall quarter, winter quarter, spring quarter, etc.	Un trimestre
57. Semester : fall semester, spring semester	Un semestre
58. A pop quiz	Un petit contrôle imprévu
59. Office hours	Les heures où un professeur est disponible pour recevoir les étudiants au bureau
60. An open-book test	Un contrôle pendant lequel les étudiants ont le droit de consulter leurs livres
61. A study group	Un groupe d'étudiants qui se rencontrent pour réviser ensemble
62. A review session	Une séance de révision avant un examen
63. A schedule	Un emploi du temps
64. Summer school	Des cours d'été
65. An endowment	Des fonds disponibles pour aider certains étudiants financièrement
66. A section	Un cours de travaux pratiques suivi en parallèle avec un cours magistral

…ENT – HOUSING

…sing terms	Vocabulaire du logement
1. to rent an apartment	Louer un appartement
2. a lease	Un bail
3. the rent	Le loyer
4. stories/floors	Les étages
5. a high-rise apartment building	Une tour
6. to show an apartment	Faire visiter un appartement
7. a vacancy	Un logement vide (et donc habitable)
8. a deposit	Une caution
9. a down-payment	Des arrhes
10. furniture (toujours singulier en anglais)	Des meubles
11. low-income housing	HLM
12. a mortgage	Une hypothèque
13. a fireplace	Une cheminée
14. a yard	Le terrain qui entoure une maison, la propriété
15. a fence	Une barrière (autour d'une maison)
16. a stove	Une cuisinière électrique (plaques chauffantes et four)
17. a carpet	Une moquette
18. a sink	Un évier, un lavabo
19. a pet	Un animal domestique
20. to mow the lawn (lawnmower)	Tondre la pelouse (tondeuse)
21. a closet	Un placard, une armoire
22. a porch	Un porche, une véranda
23. a driveway	Une allée (pour la voiture)
24. utilities	L'électricité, le gaz et l'eau (utilities bill – facture pour ceux-ci)
25. the first/ground floor	Le rez-de-chaussée (certains appellent le rez-de-chaussée *ground floor* suivi par 1, 2, etc. Par contre, d'autres commencent par *first floor*, suivi par 2, 3, etc. (2nd floor : 1er étage)
26. a sublet	Une sous-location

CHAPITRE 9

Analysez vos résultats au Diagnostic Test

1. Clé pour le Diagnostic Test
2. Scripts pour les textes à écouter, Diagnostic Test
3. Comment calculer votre résultat
4. Les critères d'évaluation

1. Clé pour le Diagnostic Test

Reading Section, Diagnostic Test

1. B
2. C.
3. D.
4. A.
5. A.
6. D.
7. A.
8. D.
9. A.
10. D.
11. D.
12. B.
13. A., C., E.
14. C.
15. C.
16. A.
17. A.
18. C.
19. D.
20. C.
21. A.
22. C.
23. C.
24. D.
25. A.
26. B., D., F.
27. A.
28. B.
29. B.
30. B.
31. A.
32. C.
33. D.
34. A.
35. B.
36. A.
37. B.
38. D.
39. B., C., F.
40. C.
41. A.
42. D.
43. B.
44. C.
45. D.
46. A.
47. D.
48. A.
49. C.
50. C.
51. B
52. 1) prescriptive
    2) descriptive
    3) prescriptive
    4) prescriptive
    5) descriptive
    6) descriptive
    7) prescriptive
    8) descriptive

Section 2 – Listening

1. b
2. | | |
   |---|---|
   | Have a cauliflower-like appearance | Cumulus |
   | Are the highest clouds at 30,000 feet | Cirrus |
   | Feathery, fibrous appearance | Cirrus |
   | Gray and thick | Stratus |
3. b
4. d
5. a
6. b, d
7. c
8. d
9. c
10. | STEPS | Number 1-4 |
    |---|---|
    | 1. Determine student's eligibility. | 3 |
    | 2. Student/parents fill out FAFSA. | 1 |
    | 3. Financial aid package offered to eligible student. | 4 |
    | 4. SAR sent out to college and financial aid agencies. | 2 |
11. a
12. c
13. c
14. a
15. Product positioning, pricing, market segment
16. c
17. b
18. Receptive – understanding sounds, picking out mother's voice. Expressive – written language, baby's crying
19. c
20. b
21. a, c
22. a, b
23. c
24. Change in climate, Hundred years war, expansion of Ottoman empire, the Black death
25. c
26. Literature, classical art, classical Greek works, architecture
27. a

28. d
29. a
30. a
31. c
32. d
33. c

Speaking Section, Diagnostic Test

Les corrigés ici sont des exemples de réponses de niveau fort.

Independent speaking #1

My 5th grade teacher, Mrs. Ivy, had a big influence on me. She was the first teacher I had who really treated us like adults… and talked to us about what it meant to be growing up. I remember that one of the things she really tried to impress on us was the value of education and learning.…She would always say that what we learned, no one could take away from us. And… um… so, learning was the most valuable thing we could do, for ourselves. She really got us to think, about what we were doing, what was important, and the consequences of our actions. I suppose that she was stricter than other teachers I had had before, and not always as nice.….but I understood, even then, that she was getting me to think about things that were really important for my future, and also introducing me to the idea of values and responsibility and thinking for myself.

Independent speaking #2

I prefer to study for final exams on my own. First of all, I know what I need to concentrate my study on. If there are some points that I am having difficulty with, I want to be able to focus on those points. In a study group, um… I am not sure that you can do that. I also need to work at my own rhythm, umm… take the time I need to make sure that I have fully understood a point before I move on. In a study group, I am afraid that I would spend time on things that I don't really need to review, if that is what the majority of the group wanted to do. In other words, I would not be able to manage my time and my study program the way I want. And… um… I also like to study very early in the morning, and I am not sure that study groups meet at that time. So, overall, I like the independence of being able to set my own time and agenda for my final exam reviews.

Integrated speaking #3

The girl is against the plan to have a combined university/public library. Because… ummmm... she thinks that the university students need to have their own library, where they are the only ummm… users and can have full access to all the resources. She also thinks that a combined library would have a lot more people using it, and so the students would not have priority. For example, she says that if more, non-university people use the library, students may not find the books they need because… uummmm… they are already checked out. Or the computers may already be in use when the students need to use them. She also says that the atmosphere in the library might change… it might become noisier, because there would be children and a lot more people, and the librarians might be busier and less available for help. So, even though she agrees that having a bigger library and longer hours sounds good, the reality of it would not be an improvement for the students.

Integrated speaking #4

Today class refers mostly to economically based classes, though in the past there were more characteristics that were taken into account. Those were occupation, education, manners, power, ownership… ummm… and a few others. The professor mentions the book « The Great Gatsby » as an example of how important the idea of inherited wealth was at the beginning of the 20th century. The upper class were those who inherited their wealth. That has changed, and today people who have high incomes are part of the upper class, even if their money was not inherited. People who earn their money are not looked down upon by those with inherited wealth, as they were in the past. Today someone who did not grow up as part of the upper class can still belong to that class by having a high income. So basically, today the idea of class is really about how much money someone earns, and not about how they grew up or where they went to school or what kind of manners they have.

Integrated speaking #5

The woman is feeling overwhelmed by campus life. She misses her family and friends. She is having a hard time getting used to living in the dorm, and… ummm… she also has a lot of work to do for school. Her friend suggests two solutions. The first is to go to the health center and get a check-up and maybe talk to a counselor. The second suggestion is to go to a student discussion group in the student union. I think that they are both good solutions… but I prefer the second one. I think the woman is lonely and um… if she could make some new friends that would help. It would probably help her to talk with other students who are feeling the same way, and maybe they could come up with some ways to make the situation better. I think that that would help her more than going to see a Doctor and getting a check-up.

Integrated speaking #6

A cell phone user has to decide whether it is better to take a prepaid plan or postpaid plan. A postpaid cell phone plan is a contract, either month-to-month or on a yearly basis. If you cancel the service before the contract is up, you are charged an early termination penalty. The contract includes a set number of minutes for local and/or long distance calls, and sometimes um… you are able to choose some phone numbers that you can call as often as you like with no added charge. These are called free numbers.

The prepaid plan is different. There is no contract… you buy a card with a certain number of minutes on it and then you can use the minutes as you need them. There is no monthly charge but the minutes cost more, and the card has an expiration date. Minutes remaining on the card after it expires are lost. So a new user needs to try to determine which plan would better suit his needs.

Writing Section, Diagnostic Test

Integrated Writing

This lecture is about the fall of the Aztec empire in 1521 as described by Diaz. His narration of what happened in the New World is radically different from what Columbus had described thirty years before.

First, the most striking difference between the two texts is the reason why Spaniards sailed to the New World. Cortés strove for power and conquest whereas Columbus had peaceful intentions of trade and thought of spreading religious faith to the Indians.

Second, the lecturer speaks about a translator constantly used by Cortés to understand and take control over the Aztec nation. This is a far cry from Columbus's idea to teach the Indians Spanish for better communication between the two peoples.

Third, it is explained in the lecture that Cortés demanded gold from the Aztecs on several occasions, which he was given. This is in direct contradiction to the poor, naked Indians described by Columbus.

Finally, there is radical opposition in the attitudes toward the inhabitants of the New World. Columbus found the native Americans innocent and with no weapons; he treated them with respect. Cortés also found the Indian chief pacific, but his reaction was to take advantage of what he considered a « weakness ». Power-thirsty, he killed as many native Americans necessary to rule the nation.

Independent Writing

The decision to pursue one's education beyond the undergraduate level involves both intellectual and economic commitments. On the one hand, higher education implies the beginning of a career of studies with hopes to advance collective knowledge in a specific field with almost no monetary compensation. On the other hand, higher education may imply important discoveries which lead to lucrative salaries later on in one's career. In the final analysis, I agree with this statement, reserving the right to define the term « a good job ».

To illustrate my point, let us imagine a Biology major who decides to pursue a higher degree in Pharmacology. If, during his doctoral studies, he makes a breakthrough discovery, he will probably end up finding a well-paid job in a large drug company, with a bright future and excellent benefits. If this person is satisfied with his situation, he will most likely say that higher education opened the door to a good job for him.

However, what if the opposite is true? Is it not feasible that the same Biology major who decides to pursue a higher degree in Pharmacology could end up working in a secluded laboratory somewhere, with a low salary? What would this person say? Would he say that higher education opened the door to a bad job for him?

I would conjecture that if he is working in his field of study, he will feel that he has a good job, no matter what the pay. In fact, is higher education not a type of insurance that one will always work in a chosen field? When one chooses higher education, does he not choose the type of work he will do for the rest of his life? If one examines the statistics carefully, those who choose their line of work in society are in a vast minority. This means, then, that higher education does open a door to a good job: it opens the door to a job in the field of one's choice.

To conclude, I would say that if « a good job » means working at a job one enjoys, I agree that the most important aspect of higher education is the choice of what a person will do for the rest of his life.

2. Scripts pour les textes à écouter, Diagnostic Test

Reading Section, pas de script

Listening Section, Texte 1, Script

NARRATOR: Listen to part of a lecture in an Earth Sciences class.

We will start our study of weather by learning about clouds.

It's a great place to start… Clouds are beautiful and inspiring. Who has not stopped to gaze at the sky on a cloudy day? How many poems and songs talk about clouds? And think of all the paintings featuring clouds. Clouds are definitely an artistic inspiration.

But, all that aside, we are here to talk about the scientific aspects of clouds. Clouds are excellent indicators of current and future weather conditions. What are they made of? How are they formed?

Well, to simplify, when air containing water vapor cools to below the dew point, the resulting moisture condenses into droplets in the atmosphere and forms clouds. Oh, by the way… Dew Point… is defined as the temperature the air would have to be cooled to in order for Saturation to occur… and Saturation is when the air is holding the maximum amount of water vapor possible at the existing temperature and pressure. But I am getting off track here…

Other ways that clouds are formed are by a reduction of pressure aloft or… um… by the mixing of warmer and cooler air currents.

Clouds have different compositions depending on where they are located in the atmosphere. Therefore, to distinguish, we refer to three levels of clouds; low-level, mid-level and high level. So… let's see the main characteristics of each one.

Low level clouds are found below 6,500 feet and are usually composed of liquid water droplets. They can contain snow and ice crystals in cold weather. Mid-level clouds are found between 6,500 and 23,000 feet and are made up of liquid water droplets during summer and a liquid droplet-ice crystal mix during winter. High-level clouds are generally found above 20,000 feet, are composed of ice crystals, and are very thin and wispy.

There is a classification system for clouds based on fundamental cloud characteristics. These are: the altitude at which they occur, color, density, shape, and… umm… degree of cover. The classification includes three basic cloud types and seven other common cloud types. The three basic cloud types are Cirrus, Cumulus and Stratus. Let's look at the basic characteristics of each type.

Cirrus clouds are thin white clouds that are separated or detached and have a feathery, fibrous appearance. They form at 30,000 feet above the earth and so… ummm… are the highest of all clouds.

Cumulus clouds are most common during the summer months. They are flat-based, billowing clouds with vertical doming. Often the top of cumulus clouds have a « cauliflower-like » appearance.

Stratus clouds are thin, sheet-like clouds, often occurring as continuous layers with some rippling, covering large portions of the sky. Stratus clouds are frequently gray and thick.

There is a lot of concern about the earth's changing climate. Clouds are a central part of this. Clouds reflect sunlight, which cools the Earth, and they also trap heat in the same way as greenhouse gases, and so warm the Earth. Different types of clouds do more of one than the other. Depending on which cloud types change, and in what ways they change, the effect of clouds on climate change will be different.

One assumption has been that as the climate warms and more water evaporates from the oceans there will be more clouds, and they will be thicker and denser. But… a warmer atmosphere needs more water vapor molecules to become saturated and to condense into clouds so we cannot anticipate how clouds will react to human-induced climate changes. An example of this would be summer and winter… summer is warmer and has higher humidity than winter but… even so… the sky is not noticeably cloudier in summer than in winter.

How do clouds fit into Global Warming? There is a lot of speculation and different theories on this. One is that the cloud composition could change drastically as the earth heats up… one scenario has low lying clouds evaporating during the day and more cirrus clouds forming as surface heat causes the air to rise. Lower clouds reflect sunlight and higher clouds absorb heat radiation so there could be more energy trapped in the atmosphere.

But… overall… the response of clouds to global warming is unpredictable, and so… clouds might change in such a way as to reduce, rather than increase, the amount of surface warming. Generally, clouds have a cooling effect as they block the light and radiation coming from the sun. On a cloudy day the sun's light and radiation bounce off the clouds and scatter back into space.

In fact, clouds are the element that trip up the computer models trying to replicate Global Warming. So… we can expect to see continued focus on clouds and research into how they are reacting as weather patterns change.

Listening Section, Texte 2

NARRATOR: Listen to the conversation between a financial aid officer and a college student:

Man: Excuse me, could you tell me where to go to get some information on financial aid, please?

Woman: I can help you with that.

Man: I need financial aid this semester and I'm not sure what is available and how to apply.

Woman: Well, there are many types of financial aid packages. First of all, are you an undergraduate or a graduate?

Man: I'm a junior.

Woman: OK, that narrows it down. Basically, there are two types of aid: based on need and based on merit. The first is mostly loans, work-study and grants, the second category includes all those and also scholarships, mostly in specific fields of study. What's your major?

Man: Well, I am currently an Engineering major but I'm considering changing over to Pre-Med.

Woman: Well, I can tell you that both of those majors are very well endowed. The first thing you have to do is fill out the Free Application for Federal Student Aid form. It's called FAFSA for short. Basically it asks about your financial situation, and your parents as well if you are still a dependent. Once you have turned it in and it has been processed, you will receive a form… ummm an SAR – that's short for Student Aid Report. That is what agencies, and we here at the financial aid office, will use to evaluate whether or not you qualify for certain kinds of financial aid.

Man: That sounds pretty involved. How long does it take?

Woman: Well, it is an annual process. You have to fill out an FAFSA every year, turn it in after January 1st, so the information is based on the tax year ending December 31st. Then you receive the SAR… you know, I already explained what that is. Then we can look at the SAR and determine where you stand and offer a package… if you're eligible, of course.

Man : Okay… but… well, it's a long way off until January. I need some help now to get through this year. What can I do ?

Woman : We really base everything on the SAR. Without that… there are a few things you can try. I'd say the best bet would be trying to get a part-time job, there are a lot of listings at the employment center.

Man : Well, that could help. But I'm afraid I need more than that. I won't be able to pay next semester's tuition without some aid. I would hate to have to take the semester off and wait until January to come back.

Woman : I understand that. Well, there are alternative loans in that case. Those are loans from banks and other financial institutions. The interest rate is higher, of course, compared… compared to Federal loans or the loan program we have here. But the advantage is that you can apply for them at any time, so… if your need is immediate, they can be helpful.

Man : I see. Well, I was wondering… do you have any sort of tuition deferment plan ?

Woman : Not exactly… but we do-sometimes- allow students to pay tuition in monthly installments, rather than all at the beginning of the semester. It's pretty rare, but if you are in good academic standing, demonstrate need, and have been here at the college for at least a year, it is something that we can consider.

Man : That would help… Maybe I could apply for that, and then in January go ahead with the regular financial aid process. How would I go about asking for tuition installments ?

Woman : Well… why don't you start by filling out this form and then we can talk more about your situation.

Man : Thanks. I'll fill it out and come back tomorrow.

Listening Section, Texte 3

NARRATOR: Listen to part of a lecture in a business class.

PROFESSOR

Today we are going to look at two important tools for getting a new business up and running – business plans and business models. Imagine… you have your idea, you've done your groundwork. Now you need to start raising capital. Before you start making appointments with investors, you need a document in hand. Something concrete that you can present to show that you have things figured out and you are not a fly-by-night operation.

First… let's start by differentiating between a business plan and a business model. A business model starts in the entrepreneur's mind… it is, quite simply, the way the business will make money. In other words, how much money and where will it be coming from? This is a projection based on the best possible research, preliminary market studies, and so on and so forth.

If put down on paper, it would be only one page long… and… ummm… would be most clearly represented by a diagram.

The business plan, on the other hand, is a long and detailed document, typically one hundred pages or more, including a lot of financial projections.

Now… umm… How do new businesses finance themselves?

Student: They borrow money… take out business loans.

Prof: Right, most new businesses apply for loans, and the lending institution – bank, credit union or even private investors – will require a business plan in order to assess the chances of the loan being paid back or the eventual return on investment.

A business plan is built on the synthesis of areas including economics, finance, marketing, strategy, operations, and entrepreneurship. A really good business plan can take an average idea and make it highly profitable. In the same way, a great idea supported by a poor business plan will not reach its full potential.

An important part of the business plan is the « place » component, if we were to use the terms of the marketing mix. In other words, will the business use franchises or company owned-outlets? If the latter, will the business own the outlet real estate or lease it? Will the strategy be direct sales or the use of retailers? And then, today, of course, there is the added option of e-commerce.

A business model is imperative when a business first gets started. But changes in the industry can also make it necessary to revamp the original business model in order to keep up with new developments. A good example of this would be the photo industry. Companies that once made their money by selling film and developing it have now had to adjust to the popularity of digital cameras. Film and developing services are a much smaller part of the market and… ummmm… may disappear completely in the not too distant future. Digital photo printing and online photo-sharing sites are taking over this market segment. A company that has always sold film, and is slow to adapt to this new way of creating photos, will not survive in the new environment.

Let's look at some of the elements of a business plan. Ummm… let's start with market segment. It's important to target the right market. That can make the difference between sales and no sales, success and failure. What are some other elements?

(student) Positioning of the product or service.

(prof) Good. Knowing the competitive environment and what they are offering is an essential part of the process. We need to know where our new offering fits into an established market, or how a new market we are trying to create will co-exist in the present environment.

(student) The financial set-up. I mean… The cost structure, the pricing, and the projected profit margins.

(prof) Another essential piece of input. Good… glad to see you have all done your reading assignment!

(student) What about… I'm not sure how to say it… the added value. You know… from the customer's perspective.

(prof) Yes, that is certainly one of the basics. What is the need that we are trying to meet with this product or service? This is one of the questions we need to answer convincingly before we can get going.

Listening Section, Texte 4

NARRATOR : Listen to part of a lecture in a Child Development class.

Let's start by looking at the difference between speech and language. Speech is the physical act of talking – the motor act of communicating through verbal expression. Speech refers to the actual process of making sounds, using such organs and structures as the lungs, vocal cords, mouth, tongue, and teeth.

Language, on the other hand… ummm… language is much broader. It encompasses the reception and… ummm… expression of information. There are two parts to speech – I'm sorry, to language. First, there is receptive language – understanding of the words and sounds we hear, or receive. The second part is using words and gestures – expressing meaning through them. This is called expressive language. It includes verbal, nonverbal and written language.

Between 2 and 5 years of age is when the most rapid speech and language development occurs. But it doesn't start then… actually, it starts before birth. Unborn babies in the uterus hear, and even respond to, familiar voices. Receptive language skills are the first learned, though… ummm… expressive language learning also begins soon after birth.

Let's look at some milestones in the first year.

In the first month, babies usually can pick out their mother's voices, and learn the different rhythms and melodies of two languages… ummm… if both are present in their environment. That falls under receptive language. In expressive language, at this age babies use undifferentiated crying, meaning… ummmm… crying that sounds the same, all the time, no matter what the need is.

Between one and four months, babies prefer « baby talk » and high-pitched voices. The sound of their mother's voice will quiet them, and they show alertness to sounds by blinking their eyes. They may react to sounds by turning towards them or becoming startled… and will make cooing sounds, usually vowel sounds.

5- to -6 month olds recognize their own names and make sounds. They start to babble and repeat sounds such as « ma-ma-ma » to get attention or express feelings. Their crying now varies with their specific needs.

7-to-9 month olds repeat sounds that they hear and mimic the rhythms they hear. They may wave « bye-bye » when they hear the words, and say « mama » and « dada ». They hear words as distinctive sounds and recognize the meaning of some facial expressions and tones of voice.

The biggest influence on a child's speech and language development is, not surprisingly, their exposure to speech and language. Parents who consistently talk and read to their offspring are setting the stage for their children's ability to successfully communicate. In contrast, children who are seldom spoken to or read to usually acquire language and speech skills later and... ummm... so learn to talk later than other children their age.

As language and speech are two independent stages, they may be individually delayed. Speech delay refers to a delay in the development or use of the mechanisms that produce speech... whereas language delay refers to a delay in the development or use of the knowledge of language. So, a child with speech delay would be producing language that would be difficult to understand. Conversely, a child with a language delay typically has not yet had the opportunity to produce speech sounds, and so is therefore likely to have a delay in speech as well.

A delay in speech development may indicate other disorders, the most common being hearing loss and autism. Other possible disorders responsible for speech delays are elective mutism, cerebral palsy, and mental retardation. Speech delay may also be a result of maturation delay or bilingualism.

Now, what are the red flags that should be cause for concern? If the child is not babbling by 18 months, not talking by age two or making sentences by age three, or is unable to tell a simple story by four to five years of age. Other reasons for concern are speech which remains largely unintelligible after age three or speech which is more than a year late compared to normal patterns of speech development. If delay is present in all aspects of development it indicates mental retardation as the cause of the speech delay.

Listening Section, Texte 5

NARRATOR: Now listen to part of a talk in an Art History class.

Today we will be delving into the background of the Renaissance. Now, this class – as you know – focuses on the art of the Renaissance. But what was happening politically and socially during the Renaissance and in the time leading up to it? In order to understand the Renaissance, we need to first get a sense of what was happening in Europe that enabled the Renaissance to take place. Studying the art of that time without the background context will not allow you to fully appreciate the Renaissance period. The Renaissance did not take place in a vacuum. It was made possible by all the change going on at that period in time...

To review, the Renaissance refers to the humanistic revival of classical art, architecture, literature, and learning that originated in Italy in the 14th century and later spread throughout Europe.

Student: I thought the Renaissance was only in Italy. Everything I remember about it is Italian... Michelangelo, the Medicis, the Sistine Chapel....

Professor: Well, that doesn't surprise me. Italy is very strongly linked to the Renaissance, and for good reason. It was the home, where the Renaissance started. Italy was the impetus for the spread of the Renaissance to other countries, as we shall see.

The Renaissance period went from the 14th to the 16th century. It started in Italy, and reached its peak there in the late 15th century. The Italian Renaissance spread and set off the Northern Renaissance and the English Renaissance.

However, in the fourteenth century there were changes that led the European economy into recession.

The Little Ice Age began... this refers to a general cooling of the climate between the years 1150 and 1460 and a very cold climate between 1560 and 1850. The change in climate caused a decline in agricultural output and led to famines, which were aggravated by the rapid population growth taking place. The Hundred Years war began between France and England, and disrupted trade in northwest Europe. The Ottoman Empire began its expansion through the East. The Black Death took its toll on the densely populated cities of Northern Italy.

At the same time, the Renaissance was slowly starting, helped along by some of the disasters I just mentioned. The expansion of the Ottoman Empire saw the arrival of wealthy and educated Greek refugees, bringing with them knowledge of classical Greek learning and many long-forgotten classical works. A third of Europe's population succumbed to the Black Death and those who were left were wealthier, better fed and had more money to spend on luxury goods, art and architecture.

In the early 15th century Europe's population began to grow again, and there was increasing demand for goods and services. The lower classes were in a favorable position to provide them, and this created a large class of bankers, merchants and skilled artisans. The influence of the church was declining.

In fact, the economic collapse was one of the essential causes of the Renaissance, as businessmen who would have invested their money had there been a favorable investment landscape, instead invested in art and culture.

Student: So the fact that the economy was doing badly actually was one of the reasons the Renaissance came about? I thought it was the opposite....

Professor: Traditionally, wealthy people at that time invested in businesses, property and more concrete investments... forgive the pun! But at this time, there were not a lot of those type of investment opportunities available. So the available money went into artistic endeavors, allowing artists to really live off their art, and so devote themselves to it. The results are some of the most famous artworks known today, for example, as you mentioned, the Sistine Chapel.

In the late 15th century the Renaissance ideal was fully recognized by the ruling classes and the aristocracy. In the early Renaissance artists were mostly of lower- or middle-class origins, were thought of as craftsmen, and received little recognition. By the later Renaissance the top artists became aristocrats, had a great deal of influence, and were able to charge high fees for their work.

Despite the massive changes brought about during the Renaissance, three quarters of the population of Northern Italy were still rural peasants. The main audience for Renaissance culture were the elite living in the cities. Artisans and guild members formed the next level of society, living comfortable lives and wielding significant power in the government.

All this to show that the Renaissance did not bring about great social or economic change, but stayed in the realm of cultural and ideological development, affecting only a small fraction of the population.

Listening Section, Texte 6

NARRATOR : Listen to part of a conversation between a professor and a student.

Woman : Good morning, Dr. Howe. I was hoping I could talk to you for a few minutes.

Man : Come in. These aren't my regular office hours, but I do have a few minutes before my next lecture.

Woman : Thanks. I'm in your Abnormal Psychology course on Tuesdays. I wanted to talk to you about the term paper.

Man : Which section are you in ? Have you talked to your T.A. ?

Woman : I'm in the Friday morning section with Karen Carlson. I have talked to her, I went to her office hours last week… but I'm still not clear on a few things. You see, I… well, I didn't do as well as I had hoped on the mid-term… and I really need to bring my grade up. So I'm counting a lot on my term paper to do that.

Man : Yes, well the term paper does count for 30 % of your final grade. What topic have you chosen ?

Woman : I'm focusing on the Schizophrenic personality. I've done a lot of research but I haven't defined my main thesis yet.

Man : Well, the due date is approaching quickly. You don't want to spend much more time deciding on what you want to focus on, you need to be in the writing phase soon. There's the final exam to study for as well…

Woman : That's the problem… I'm already starting to feel overwhelmed. I'm carrying a full load this term... 18 units… I have an enormous amount of studying to do. And of course I will have all those final exams to cram for. So I was wondering if there is any way I can do some work now that would count for extra credit… you know, so that if my grade on the final exam is a little low… I could make up for it… It's important that I maintain at least a 3.0 GPA.

Man : I understand your concern. But I'm not in favor of extra credit projects. They usually are not very useful, either for you or as a way to evaluate your work in the course. The final exam covers all of the coursework so it is the best indication of what you've retained. Any extra credit work you could do would only be a research exercise. I'm not sure it would be fair to get extra points for that.

Woman : I see what you mean. But… I guess I really need to concentrate on preparing for the final exam. Could you give me any tips on the best way to do that ?

Man : The best thing to do would be to meet with your T.A. She can help you to go over the syllabus and figure out what to concentrate your review on. I believe the sections also meet for review sessions, if enough students are interested.

Woman : That would be a big help. I'll go to Ms. Carlson's office hours tomorrow. Thanks so much for your help.

Man : Anytime. If I can give you any more tips on preparing for the end of the course, please come by again. By the way… don't forget that participation in your section counts for 25 %... that's an important part of the final grade.

Woman : Oh, I haven't forgotten about that ! I've made a real effort to participate at each meeting. The section has been a great complement to the lecture… we have talked in-depth about a lot of the material and really gotten into some of the underlying theory. I've really enjoyed the class, both the lecture and the section. I plan to take more psychology classes next semester. Thank you for your time, Dr. Howe.

Speaking Section, Texte 1, Script

NARRATOR : Please listen to the question carefully.

Think of a teacher who has had an influence on you. Describe the qualities this teacher possessed and in what way he or she influenced you. Provide details and examples to support your explanation.

NARRATOR : Please begin speaking now.

Speaking Section, Texte 2

NARRATOR : Please listen to the question carefully.

Some students prefer to study for final exams on their own and others prefer to attend group study sessions. Which do you think is better and why ?

NARRATOR : Please begin speaking now.

Speaking Section, Texte 3

Narrator : Now listen to a student who is speaking at a student forum about the proposed joint library :

It sounds great to have a bigger library with more resources and longer hours, but let's not forget that there will be a lot more people, um….patrons using the library and we have to consider what that will mean for students…..Will we have priority for certain books ? If not, we may end up not being able to check out the books we need because they are already out. Or… um... not being able to use the internet computers to do research because there are so many people waiting to use them. I think a University library has to be for the school's students and not for the general public. The library we have now is a great place to study – it's quiet and the librarians are always available for help. That would change if the library started to serve the general public too – I mean, there would be small children making noise, and the librarians would have to assist other patrons and not be as available for the University students.

Narrator: The student expresses her opinion about the university's proposal for a library. State her opinion and explain the reasons she gives for holding that opinion.

Please begin speaking now.

Speaking Section, Texte 4

NARRATOR: Now listen to part of a lecture on this topic in a sociology class

Today we are going to talk about the characteristics of the classes in modern capitalist societies. There is a lot of disagreement over the theory of class, but much less over the, um, characteristics of class. These are occupation, education, income, manners, net worth, power, ownership, politics and reputation.

To give a short, um, overview, we can say that the upper class has traditionally been those who have inherited their wealth. This characteristic was of utmost importance as recently as the first part of the 20th century, as illustrated in « The Great Gatsby ». If you recall the book, those who earned their fortunes, referred to as « new money », were considered the... the underclass and were looked down upon by those with inherited wealth. Today class refers almost exclusively to economically based classes, whereas in the past more characteristics were taken into account. Today those at the highest income levels, regardless of what class they grew up in, are part of the upper class. Those who have worked their way into high paying managerial jobs fall into the upper middle class, regardless of their education or manners. The middle class includes professionals and those in technical occupations, shopkeepers, farmers and so on. So... manual laborers and semi-or unskilled workers who earn moderate or low wages make up the working class. The permanently unemployed and underemployed make up the « underclass ».

Narrator: The professor describes the changes in the concept of class and its characteristics in the 20th century. Explain the main changes and give examples.

Speaking Section, Texte 5

Narrator : Now listen to a conversation between a student and her friend.

Man : Hi, Karen. How's it going?

Woman : OK, I guess.

Man : Anything wrong?

Woman : Well… I really miss my family and friends back home. It's hard living in the dorm. And… I… I have so much studying to do, papers to write.

Man : College life can be pretty difficult, the first year.

Woman : Well, I was really excited about going away and living on campus. I never imagined that I would miss home… and my family.

Man : Are you taking care of yourself? You know, eating regularly and exercising, and getting enough sleep?

Woman ; Lately it seems like all I've had time to do is study.

Man : Maybe you should go to the Health center. You could just get a check-up, you know, to see if you need vitamins… or anything. And it might help to talk to one of the counselors.

Woman : You think so? I wouldn't know what to say.

Man : I think they're used to this kind of situation. They could probably give you some good advice.

Woman : I don't know… I feel kind of uncomfortable going to talk to a counselor.

Man : Hey, you know they hold student discussion groups in the student union. Meeting other students in similar situations might help.

Woman : Well… yes, making some new friends might help. I'll go by the student union and find out about it.

Narrator : The students talk about two possible solutions to the woman's problem. First describe the problem and then say which of the two solutions you prefer and why.

Speaking Section, Texte 6

Now listen to a talk about cellphone plans.

One of the decisions facing a new cell phone user is whether to use a prepaid or a postpaid plan.

Most wireless service is sold on a contract basis, with contracts ranging from month-to-month to one, two or three year contracts. Plans include a fixed number of minutes, local and/or long-distance, and often a perk known as « free » numbers – meaning you can call a certain number of pre-designated phone numbers as much as you like, with no added charge.

One of the disadvantages of the contract is that there is an early termination penalty, regardless of the reason for terminating service. The cancellation fee can vary from a flat fee to a charge for every month remaining on your contract.

The prepaid cell phone plan avoids the problem of signing a long term contract by providing a sort of cell phone debit card – you buy a card with a pre-determined number of minutes on it and then use it as you like. The advantage is that there is no contract and no monthly fee. Of course, you will pay more per minute of airtime, and usually there is an expiration date for the card. Any minutes remaining on the card after the expiration date are forfeited.

Narrator: Using points from the talk, explain the decisions facing a new cellphone user.

Writing Section, Script

Well, let's begin by saying that pages and pages have been written to describe the Spanish colonization of the Americas. Today, though, we will concentrate on the work of Bernal Diaz del Castillo, entitled The Conquest of New Spain, although the title in Spanish is « Historia verdadera », or the « true story » of The Conquest of New Spain. This work is a description of the fall of the Aztec empire in 1521. The « true story » aspect needs to be emphasized, since the author, Diaz, that's D-I-A-Z, wrote this story to deny what was for him other « false stories » which praised only Hernan Cortés as the leader of the Spanish conquest. He wrote at age eighty-four to recount his own experiences as one of Hernan Cortés's soldiers.

Well, let's see now, it is in fact mostly thanks to this man that we know so much today about « la Malinche », the slave girl picked up by Cortés, who translated from the Nahuatl and Mayan languages. Diaz writes, quote « Without her help, we would not have understood the language of New Spain and Mexico » enquote. She was constantly at Cortes's side, and her translations helped Cortés develop war strategies to defeat and kill the Aztec nation.

Oh, by the way, Diaz also relates in detail Cortés's demands for gifts of gold which were immediately met by Montezuma, the Aztec chief. When Cortés then captured Montezuma, and asked for a ransom in gold, this demand was equally met by the Aztec community.

Diaz also relates the death of Montezuma inflicted by Cortes's soldiers. Quote « Montezuma told them to stop the wars and to leave his city... and they threw three big stones at him, one at his head, another at his arm, and another at a leg... and then, they came to say that he had died. » enquote

Diaz's book allows readers to relive one of the bloodiest chapters in Spanish colonization.

3. Comment calculer votre résultat

Il est impossible de calculer votre résultat exact au TOEFL iBT à partir du diagnostic test de ce livre. L'ETS, concepteur du TOEFL iBT, ne révèle jamais les barèmes qu'il utilise pour certaines sections, et peut les changer à tout moment. Cependant, ce diagnostic test a été conçu pour couvrir un très grand nombre des questions linguistiques qui se trouvent au programme du TOEFL iBT. Le diagnostic test de ce livre constitue donc une révision complète du programme.

D'ailleurs, la nature même de l'examen rend impossible le calcul exact de votre résultat au diagnostic test. Il faudrait des correcteurs pour noter vos rédactions et vos réponses orales. La moitié du TOEFL iBT est évaluée par des examinateurs.

Malgré l'impossibilité de calculs exacts, une série de tableaux et de renseignements est fournie par l'ETS pour mieux interpréter les performances au TOEFL iBT. En voici quelques-uns.

4. Les critères d'évaluation

Tout d'abord, examinons la Writing Section. Chaque candidat écrit deux rédactions, notées de 0 à 5 chacune. Ensuite, une moyenne des deux notes est calculée. Le barème suivant est appliqué à cette moyenne pour que le résultat se situe entre 0 et 30 :

La moyenne des deux rédactions	Equivalence selon le barème
5,00	30
4,75	29
4,5	28
4,25	27
4,00	25
3,75	24
3,5	22
3,25	21
3,00	20
2,75	18
2,5	17
2,25	15
2,00	14
1,75	12
1,5	11
1,25	10
1,00	8
0,75	7
0,50	5
0,25	4
0,00	0

Pour cette section du TOEFL iBT, le barème est donc clair. Mais comment arriver à la note du départ ? Pour cela, l'ETS fournit la grille d'interprétation suivante :

Grille d'interprétation : WRITING SECTION

Note	Integrated	Independent
5	La réponse comporte les renseignements importants de la conférence et les compare au contenu du passage écrit de manière cohérente. Réponse organisée, sans trop de fautes.	La réponse répond au sujet, est bien organisée, cohérente, montre une progression, utilise du vocabulaire varié, comporte très peu d'erreurs de grammaire.
4	La plupart des renseignements importants de la conférence sont exprimés et comparés à ceux du passage écrit, mais il y a quelques lacunes ou imprécisions. Des fautes plus nombreuses.	Répond au sujet, mais certaines idées sont peu élaborées. Plus de fautes linguistiques, mais qui ne nuisent pas à la compréhension.
3	Certains renseignements de la conférence ont été compris, mais une idée essentielle est omise. Les comparaisons avec le passage manquent de clarté. Les fautes sont plus fréquentes.	Répond au sujet, mais le choix des mots n'est pas clair. Expression des idées très vague. Choix de syntaxe et de vocabulaire très vague.
2	La réponse comporte quelques idées de la conférence, mais pas les idées essentielles. La comparaison des deux textes est erronée. Fautes linguistiques graves ; expression limitée.	Développe très peu le sujet. Organisation insuffisante. Aucune illustration pour soutenir ses idées. Choix de mots inapproprié ; fautes linguistiques graves.
1	La réponse ne comporte presque aucun renseignement de la conférence. Expression incompréhensible à cause d'un niveau linguistique bas.	Manque d'organisation. Aucun détail. Manque de développement. Fautes graves et fréquentes de structure.
0	Rédaction blanche. Rédaction copiée du texte à l'écran. Rédaction écrite en langue étrangère.	Hors sujet. Rédaction copiée du texte à l'écran. Rédaction écrite en langue étrangère.

La même démarche est valable pour la Speaking Section. Chacune des six interventions orales est notée de 0 à 4 points. Ensuite, une moyenne des six notes est calculée. Le barème suivant est ensuite appliqué :

La moyenne des six interventions orales	Equivalence selon le barème
4,00	30
3,83	29
3,66	28
3,5	27
3,33	26
3,16	24
3,00	23
2,83	22
2,66	20
2,5	19
2,33	18
2,16	17
2,00	15
1,83	14
1,66	13
1,5	11
1,33	10
1,16	9
1,00	8
0,83	6
0,66	5
0,50	4
0,33	3
0,16	1
0,00	0

Comme pour la Writing Section, une grille d'interprétation est fournie par l'ETS pour déterminer les notes :

Grille d'interprétation : SPEAKING SECTION

Résultat	Description générale	Débit	Structure	Développement du sujet
4	Discours cohérent et intelligible ; le candidat s'exprime avec facilité et ne cherche presque jamais ses mots.	Le candidat parle couramment, avec clarté. Quelques difficultés de prononciation ou d'intonation qui ne nuisent pas à la clarté générale.	Bonne maîtrise de grammaire et de vocabulaire, avec automatismes. Quelques petites erreurs qui ne modifient pas le sens du message.	Développement cohérent des idées exprimées. Progression ou relations claires des idées.
3	Discours cohérent en général, mais avec des lacunes en expression. Une ou plusieurs idées ne sont pas suffisamment bien développées.	Le candidat parle couramment, avec clarté, mais les difficultés en prononciation ou en intonation demandent un effort de la part de l'interlocuteur.	En général, maîtrise satisfaisante de grammaire et de vocabulaire. Toutefois, certains choix de mots sont imprécis ou il y a des erreurs de grammaire qui n'influent pas sur la communication générale.	Les idées sont claires, mais parfois limitées en développement. Relations entre idées parfois pas claires.
2	Expression suffisante, mais limitée. Une partie du discours peut manquer de clarté.	Discours intelligible en général, mais l'interlocuteur doit faire des efforts pour comprendre l'articulation, l'intonation, le rythme de la phrase.	Usage de structures simples, qui empêchent une expression complète. Maîtrise limitée de grammaire et de vocabulaire.	Seulement des idées de base, élaborées avec peu de détails. Relations entre idées assez floues.
1	Discours limité en cohérence et en contenu.	Des difficultés régulières de prononciation et d'intonation qui gênent l'interlocuteur. Des pauses, des hésitations fréquentes.	Expression très limitée par lacunes de grammaire, vocabulaire. Relations entre idées très limitées.	Discours qui consiste en idées de base sans développement particulier. Discours qui consiste de phrases répétées.
0	Pas d'expression.			

Pour de plus amples renseignements au sujet de ces critères, visitez le site www.toefl.org, le site officiel du TOEFL iBT.

Les barèmes correspondant aux sections Reading et Listening ne sont pas communiqués par l'ETS. Il ne faut surtout pas imaginer qu'une réponse vaut un certain nombre de points. Comme pour les autres sections, une note de base est trouvée, et un barème est appliqué. Ce qu'on peut examiner, en revanche, est le tableau des pourcentiles de résultats. Pour la Reading Section, la médiane se trouve entre 17 et 18 points (sur 30). Un tiers des candidats obtiendra en dessous de 15 points, et un tiers obtiendra au-dessus de 20 points. Pour la Listening Section, la médiane est entre 18 et 19. Un tiers des candidats obtiendra au-dessus de 21 points, et un tiers en dessous de 15 points. Les tableaux complets correspondant à ces chiffres se trouvent sur le site officiel du TOEFL iBT (www.toefl.org).

Quant au résultat total, la médiane du TOEFL iBT se situe entre 68 et 69 points. Un tiers des candidats obtiendra au-dessus de 79 points, et un tiers en dessous de 56 points. Voici le tableau officiel des résultats par rapport au classement en pourcentiles :

TOTAL	POURCENTILE	TOTAL	POURCENTILE	TOTAL	POURCENTILE	TOTAL	POURCENTILE
120	100,0	89	77,9	58	35,6	28	5,7
119	99,98	88	76,9	57	34,6	27	5,2
118	99,9	87	76,1	56	33,5	26	4,7
117	99,9	86	74,5	55	32,7	25	4,2
116	99,8	85	73,1	54	31,2	24	3,7
115	99,5	84	71,9	53	29,9	23	3,2
114	99,3	83	70,6	52	28,6	22	2,9
113	98,7	82	69,1	51	27,4	21	2,5
112	98,2	81	67,8	50	26,5	20	2,1
111	97,6	80	66,2	49	25,6	19	1,7
110	96,8	79	64,8	48	24,5	18	1,2
109	96,1	78	63,5	47	23,2	17	0,8
108	95,5	77	62,0	46	22,1	16	0,7
107	95,1	76	60,5	45	20,9	15	0,6
106	94,2	75	59,0	44	19,5	14	0,4
105	93,6	74	57,4	43	18,8	13	0,4
104	92,9	73	56,3	42	17,8	12	0,3
103	92,3	72	54,6	41	16,7	11	0,2
102	91,1	71	53,7	40	15,8	10	0,2
101	90,1	70	52,3	39	14,8	9	0,1
100	89,0	69	51,0	38	14,2	8	0,04
99	88,3	68	49,6	37	13,1	7	0,04
98	87,3	67	48,3	36	12,2	6	
97	86,6	66	46,7	35	11,1	5	
96	85,9	65	45,5	34	10,1	4	
95	85,0	64	44,3	33	9,2	3	
94	83,8	63	42,7	32	8,5	2	
93	82,8	62	41,6	31	7,8	1	
92	82,0	61	40,4	30	7,4	0	
91	81,0	60	38,9	29	6,5		
90	79,7	59	37,4				

Une dernière remarque : attention à un très mauvais raisonnement. Penser qu'on peut rattraper une faiblesse avec un excellent résultat dans une autre section est dangereux. Par exemple, si la compréhension auditive est difficile pour un candidat, il pourrait être tenté de se dire « je vais me rattraper avec la rédaction » afin d'obtenir un meilleur résultat global. Cela ne marche pas forcément vis-à-vis des écoles.

Voici quelques exemples de résultats exigés par des écoles :

Brigham Young University

Total Score : 85

Reading, 21	Speaking, 22
Listening, 21	Writing, 21

Purdue University

Total Score : 77

Reading, 19	Speaking, 18
Listening, 14	Writing, 18

University of California – Berkeley

Total Score : 68

Reading, 17	Speaking, 17
Listening, 16	Writing, 18

University of Virginia

Total Score : 90

Reading, 23	Speaking, 22
Listening, 23	Writing, 22

On constate tout de suite qu'il y a des résultats minima pour chaque section, et qu'un résultat total satisfaisant n'est pas forcément suffisant pour être admis dans une école (pour d'autres résultats exigés par des écoles, consultez le site www toefl. org).

CHAPITRE 10

Les réponses aux exercices

1. Clé pour les exercices
2. Script des textes écoutés, exercices
3. Sujets de rédaction supplémentaires

1. Clé pour les exercices

Voici les « bonnes réponses aux questions »

Reading Section, Exercice 1, La signification du vocabulaire à partir des préfixes, des suffixes, et des racines

1. F
2. I
3. J
4. H
5. G
6. E
7. B
8. K
9. D
10. L
11. A
12. C

Reading Section, Exercice 2, Révision de la signification du vocabulaire

1. B
2. C
3. A
4. D
5. C
6. B
7. A
8. C
9. C
10. D

Reading Section, Exercice 3, La paraphrase

1. D
2. A
3. C

Reading Section, Exercice 4, Les antécédents

1. B
2. D
3. A
4. B
5. A

Reading Section, Exercice 5, Les exceptions

1. A
2. B
3. D

Reading Section, Exercice 6, La compréhension et les sous-entendus

1. D
2. C
3. D
4. D
5. B
6. D
7. D
8. C

Reading Section, Exercice 7, Les résumés de texte et les tableaux

Texte 1

1. Communication is the basic source for stating advertising goals.
2. These goals can be checked by survey.
3. Experts used to judge the effects of advertising through sales, but not anymore.

Texte 2

1. Gray hair grows because of genetic reasons.
2. All of a person's hair follicles are intact three months before birth.
3. Hair is a non-organic material.

Reading Section, Exercice 8, L'insertion d'une phrase

1. L'insertion après la troisième phrase.
2. L'insertion après la troisième phrase.
3. L'insertion après la quatrième phrase.

Writing Section, Exercice 1, Phrasal verbs

1. a	6. b	11. a
2. a	7. b	12. a
3. b	8. b	13. b
4. b	9. a	14. b
5. a	10. a	15. b

Writing Section, Exercice 2, Accent américain

1. a	6. b
2. a	7. a
3. b	8. b
4. b	9. a
5. a	10. b

Writing Section, Exercice 3, Les «faux amis»

1. b	6. a
2. b	7. b
3. b	8. b
4. a	9. b
5. b	10. b

Writing Section, Exercice 5, Résumé de texte 2

1. In the Bay of Fundy (Gulf of Maine), where tides are highest in the world, the time for a wave to travel down the bay and back coincides with the time from one high tide to another.
2. When the wind blows on the ocean, friction and pressure cause waves and energy is transferred to the water.
3. Ocean surface particles move in elliptical motion with the waves.

Résumé de texte

The lecture discusses waves and tidal resonance. The Bay of Funday in the Gulf of Maine, where tides are the highest in the world, experiences tidal resonance in which two times coincide: the time for a wave to travel down the bay and back and the time from one high tide to another.

The phemonenon of waves is also described. Friction and pressure are applied to the ocean by the wind which causes waves and a transfer of energy to the water. Particles on the ocean's surface then move in elliptical motion, back and forth and up and down.

Writing Section, Exercice 6

The lecture is about Arnold Schoenberg, the founder of atonality, which is a sort of revolution against the tonal hierarchy in traditional music. Although the reading states that he began the twelve-tone system, the lecture discusses his opposition to the choice of the word «atonal», which means «without tone». In fact, he would have preferred the word «pan-tonal music» for his compositions.

The passage acclaims Schoenberg as the father of a new movement, whereas the lecture describes a concert in 1913 in which the police had to be called, due to a rowdy audience objecting to the radical, dissonant music played by the orchestra. It goes on to say that the general reaction to Schoenberg's music is usually black or white, according to one's willingness to accept dissonance.

Both texts mention Pierrot Lunaire, however, contrary to what the lecture says, the passage describes it as a major musical composition. The lecture claims that this half-spoken work is bizarre and unattractive to audiences.

The standpoints of the two passages contradict each other most in their respective conclusions. The reading passage states that Schoenberg is an influential modern composer, whereas the lecture calls atonality one of the two great errors of the 20th century.

Writing Section, Exercice 7, Des arguments directs et précis

1. Second, I believe History is unimportant because of the abundance of facts about the past a student finds during research. How can the year Thomas Edison went to school be linked to the many current events of our daily lives ?
2. Finally, I support studies of the basics of History because certain facts can relate to present situations. For instance, all young people should be required to learn about World War II and its atrocities as a necessary lesson about man's behavior.

Writing Section, Exercice 8, Des mots de structure

1. A
2. D
3. B
4. C
5. C
6. B

Writing Section, Exercice 9, Le rajout des mots de structure (des réponses à plusieurs possibilités)

1. It is obvious that knowing if there is life somewhere in outer space has been intriguing mankind for centuries. In my view, there is definitely life on other planets. I am convinced that other beings will some day come to Earth to conquer our planet, and we humans will have to bow down to new leaders. The fact remains that we can see pictures of UFO's in the newspaper every day. To conclude, I believe that our day of reckoning is yet to come.
2. In my opinion, there is no possible life on other planets. As far as I am concerned, man is God's uniquely created being, and thus, there is no other planet in our solar system on which humans could survive. As a matter of fact, if there were life on another planet, wouldn't we know it by now ? In conclusion, that is why man has to be the only creature in the universe.

Writing Section, Exercice 10, Mise en application

This statement is the expression of a piece of advice, explaining that one's professional and private lives should be kept separate at all times. On the one hand, the running of a company requires strict adherence to a behavioral code in order to abide by the rules of business. On the other hand, pleasure implies relaxation, fun, and just the opposite of discipline. Taking all aspects into account, despite the inevitable intertwining of the two worlds at times, I believe that professional and private activities should be conducted as two different entities.

First of all, it is upon entering the working world that a person learns the rules of professional conduct. It is the survival of business which curbs the amount of pleasure to be admitted. For instance, a company cannot survive if the staff drinks too much alcohol on the job; however, a small glass of champagne at a retirement party is a common practice in business. So, it can be observed that business and pleasure do mix, but only to a certain extent.

As a matter of fact, it is easy to observe mixtures of business and pleasure in everyday life. With the invention of modern communication devices, like cellphones, e-mail, and answer machines, it is virtually impossible not to transgress boundaries between the two. It is as common for a person to receive personal phone calls while working, as it is to receive professional e-mails at home. Of course, such mixtures, if kept short, are considered acceptable details. However, if professional calls and messages are not dealt with as quickly as possible in the presence of customers, companies can lose their business because these customers will go to competitors. Thus, from a professional point of view, the mixture of business and pleasure has its limits, due to the risk involved.

Another way to justify my point of view is a look at the other side of the coin. Who wants to talk about business matters on Saturday night at a party or a concert? Apart from telling a few company stories at a party, the hours of private life are to be spent relaxing, not going over the company's figures. As the saying goes, all work and no play makes John a dull boy. Therefore, from a personal point of view, mixing business with pleasure is acceptable for a short time, but too much can be very boring.

In conclusion, my stance on this issue is that business and pleasure do not mix by their respective natures. Although there are many small meetings of the two worlds and even if they sometimes mix superficially, the necessary discipline for business along with the relaxed aspect of private life do not make the two fundamentally compatible.

2. Script pour les textes écoutés, exercices

Reading Section, pas de script

Listening Section

Exercice 1

NARRATOR : The following practice lecture is from a History class. Listen and take notes.

Today we are starting our study of the Industrial Revolution. Now, to set things straight, there were two Industrial Revolutions. The first Industrial Revolution took place in Great Britain at the end of the 18th century. The second began at the end of the 19th century in the United States. I'll give some background on the British Industrial Revolution, but my main focus will be the American version.

The Industrial Revolution refers to economic and social changes which were the result of the introduction of new technologies of production. The Industrial Revolution brought about a major shift in society – before it occurred, societies were essentially agricultural ; after the Industrial Revolution, society was dominated by industry and manufacturing. The consequences were both positive and negative, as we shall see.

The British Industrial Revolution followed the rapid adaptation of three new technologies – the steam machine, which used coal, machines for spinning thread and weaving cloth, which were driven by steam, and furnaces to make iron ore into finished metal, also using coal.

In the United States it was the result of innovations in the production of metals and other materials, machinery, chemicals and foodstuffs.

There were three major developments responsible for the 2nd Industrial Revolution. The most important one was the completion of modern transportation and communication networks. These were railroad, steamship, telegraph and cable. The second one was the advent of electricity in the 1880s. Widespread electricity made many things possible – power, urban transportation, better illumination in the workplace and the home. The third development was the application of science to industrial processes.

In 18th and 19th century England there was plenty of skilled labor so the new machines did not replace workers, rather the machines made work more efficient. In America the growing nation had an inadequate work force and so machines helped to supplement it.

The Industrial Revolution marked huge progress for industry but the social consequences....well, they were not so bright. One of these consequences was urban growth. People left rural areas and came to cities to find work. This new working class had poor living conditions. Due to low wages children began to enter the workforce, toiling in factories alongside adults to help support their families.

The effect of the Industrial Revolution on women's work is interesting to note. Before the Industrial Revolution, American women did much of the work necessary for family survival. Yarn, cloth, candles and food were manufactured by women in the home. By 1790 water-powered machinery was put into use in the manufacture of cloth, taking over from women's hand labor. Early mills increased the value of women's household labor through outwork. This refers to the practice of contracting work out to women to do at home. As late as 1820, more than two-thirds of cloth manufactured in the US were produced by women working at home.

The use of outwork declined after the first textile factory opened in Waltham Massachusetts in 1814. The success of this factory brought about the development of the urban working class,... umm... and the network of single-industry towns. Lowell, Massachusetts became the leading textile center in America. The factory workers were single, white, native-born women from middle-class New England farms. They worked over 70 hours a week at low wages.

Most women working factory jobs in the first decades of industrialization were single. Immigrant and working-class wives and mothers were more often outworkers. Outwork was a very exploitative form of employment. Outworkers had limited mobility and bargaining power and so were often taken advantage of by their employers who cut and withheld wages.

One of the consequences of the Industrial Revolution for women is that their traditional work in the home was devalued. « Real » labor became work that had a concrete market value. The household was seen as a place of leisure and consumption, no longer one of labor and production.

Exercice 2

NARRATOR: The following practice conversation is between two students. Listen and take notes.

Man: Hi, I'm calling about the ad you have up in the student union. Are you still looking for a roommate?

Woman: Yeah, we are. Let me explain the situation. There are three of us – 3 students – renting a house and we need a 4th. You would have your own bedroom and a shared bathroom. We're 2 women and a man right now.

Man: I see. Are you all full-time students?

Woman: I am, but Amanda and John work part-time and go to school part-time. What about yourself?

Man: I'm a full-time student and I also work on the week-ends. My name is Dave Carter, by the way.

Woman: Hi. I'm Ellie Cartwright. So, where are you living right now?

Man: Well, I'm in the dorm… since the beginning of the semester. But I'm finding that there is really a lot of noise and partying. It's really hard to study… for me. So I decided I would rather live off-campus even if it means having no food service and not being as close to the library and all that. So… what I am wondering is… how quiet is it at your place? I mean, are you guys pretty studious? Or do you party a lot?

Woman: Wow, it's so hard to even get a place in the dorm… and you want to give yours up! I understand though, all that noise would make me nuts. I can tell you that in this house we are all really serious. This year we have had a couple of parties on the weekends, but we all have to agree on that. I'm pre-med and I have a huge amount of work. Amanda is an Engineering major, so ditto. And John is a grad student and he… um… he's hoping to finish his thesis this year. So we really hit the books most of the time.

Man: That sounds good. Could you tell me a little more about the arrangement. Like how is the rent split, and the utilities. What about meals – are they group style or every man for himself?

Woman : Well, We split the rent four ways as we each have our own bedroom. Utilities, the same. We have had some common meals but we have pretty different eating styles, so we tend… usually… to just fend for ourselves.

Man : What about cleaning ? I have to say I'm pretty neat and clean…

Woman : Well, that is sometimes an issue. We are supposed to have chores but sometimes they don't get done. We hold house meetings once a week and housework has come up several times. I'm not sure how we are going to handle that.

Man : How far is the house from campus ?

Woman : About 20 minutes by foot. Umm… what's your major and what year are you in ?

Man : I'm a Sophmore, Economics. I transferred from State.

Woman : OK. Well, if you're interested… why don't you come by tonight ? Uuummm… do you think… could you bring your student body card ? We just want to make sure that we really have a fellow student as a roommate. With the housing shortage a lot of working people are looking to rent rooms, too.

Man : Oh, OK. Sure. So how does the interview process work ? I mean, how do you decide who to accept as a roommate ?

Woman : Well, we all meet you… together… and then you can ask whatever questions you have… we'll show you the house… and then we'll ask some questions… you know, to see if we all seem compatible. Then we talk it over and we'll get back to you tomorrow.

Man : OK. And when could I move in, assuming I get chosen ?

Woman : Well, the room is empty now. Our last roommate dropped out. She paid this month's rent, though… so you could start moving in as soon as you want… the month is up next week in any case. How does it work with your dorm room ? Don't you have to pay for the whole semester in advance ?

Man : Yes, but as there's a waiting list to get into the dorms, it's not a problem. They select someone and that person just reimburses me what I already paid and the room transfers over to his name.

Woman : Great. Well, see you tonight. Does 7pm work? We're at 225 Grant Road, just off of Harley.

Man : OK, great. See you then.

Speaking Section, pas de script

Writing Section

Exercice 1, Phrasal verbs

1. In case there is a little confusion about Leonardo Da Vinci's theory, let's break it down.
2. The explanation for the failure to perform this scientific experiment is not complicated. It really boils down to a lack of funding.
3. Jonas Salk made an important breakthrough as the inventor of the first polio vaccine.
4. Professor Wood brought up the term paper due just before spring break.
5. A serious student always highlights important ideas he comes across in his readings.
6. After Professor LePage's lecture on elasticity, there were numerous follow-up questions.
7. No Anthropology student wants to do his research over.
8. Has the class figured out why the answer comes to 128,000 ?
9. Although it was clearly marked on the syllabus, Dr. Brown kept putting off the test.
10. We'll wrap up today's class with a slide presentation about the Neanderthal period.
11. Look into reserving the overhead projector with Mrs. Marciniak, the librarian.
12. Although Ernest Hemingway was not yet a confirmed author when he first lived in Paris, he had definitely narrowed down the possibilities of the writing style he would use in his later works.
13. I could go on about George Washington Carver, but this class is drawing to an end.
14. Last week, we left off at Attila and the Huns and their travels through Europe.
15. Today's exam will be handed back next week.

Exercice 2, L'accent américain

1. Did you pay your rent for April ?
2. My utilities bill is sky high.
3. Could we get some hot dogs ?
4. What's the matter ? Haven't you found an internship yet ?
5. Would you like some more butter ?
6. Send your resume as soon as possible.
7. What did you think of the man from Arkansas ?
8. I have got to get some gas.
9. What had he done to deserve it ?
10. Are you going to the mall with Barb ?

Exercice 3, Les « faux amis »

1. Actually, earthquakes occur every day.
2. Last night, George assisted the magic show.
3. Mike is a confirmed bachelor.
3. There will be a delay of 20 minutes.
3. Jayne passed her exam.
3. They realized the market study was accurate.
3. Jack is the most sensible boy I've ever met.
3. Her grandfather is the sympathetic type.
3. Mathew was on stage last week.
10. Gone With The Wind, by Margaret Michell, is in the library.

Exercice 4, Résumé de texte 1

In 1998, there was a bid in the UK which encouraged children to take their parents to court so that insurance companies would have to foot accident bills. The way it went for the law firm which made the bid is that any accident happening to a child would enable that child to sue his parents for neglect. Unstable car seats, wobbly high chairs, insecure cribs, you name it: every reason would be good enough to find a way to bring parents to court. If children fell, they would claim that their parents did not take the necessary steps to prevent this accident from happening.

You must admit that the thought is scary for some, and enticing for others. Uh, the idea of even doing this is pretty horrible to most parents. Can you imagine having your name splashed all over the newspaper because your

son or daughter is suing you? What a nightmare! But in this case, the law firm had thought things out first. Believe it or not, the child would end up just suing the parents'insurance company, and the parents'name would just be used for legal papers. Besides, most of this type of case is settled out of court, so parents wouldn't need to worry about their reputation.
You can imagine that this law firm caused a lot of hullabaloo. The Federation of Insurance Lawyers got into the act by saying that there was only one real culprit behind this idea in the first place. Certain lawyers just wanted to drum up more business by encouraging court cases and describing easy-win situations to customers. For the Federation, such dishonest practice was a way for these lawyers to get richer by breaking down the family unit. Besides, parents who did this would end up paying higher insurance premiums, anyway.

Exercice 5, Résumé de texte 2

OK, today we're going to discuss waves and tidal resonance. I'm sure you're well aware that you were supposed to have read chapter 4 on tidal resonance for today's class. So, I suppose that if we study the example of the northeast corner of the Gulf of Maine, between the provinces of Nova Scotia and New Brunswick, the Bay of Fundy, this should ring a bell to you from your reading. I am referring, of course, to the bay with the highest tides in the world. Now, what does tidal resonance mean if applied to the Bay of Fundy? Well, and I hope this is review for you all, tidal resonance means that two times coincide perfectly. What are these two times? Well, there is the time for a large wave to enter and travel down the bay, experience reflection, and travel back to the mouth. The time for this to happen is exactly the time lapsed from one high tide to the next.
Of course, here, the term « wave » can be defined as a disturbance which propagates through water and the term « reflection » means a change in direction of a wave due to its hitting a reflective surface. The reflective surface here, of course, is land.
Right, so all these concepts should be review to you all. Today, let's talk about ocean surface waves alone. These waves occur on the surface when the wind blows. Friction and pressure from the wind cause a disturbance on the water, and in fact, there is actually a transfer of energy. The water gains energy because of this friction. The surface particles then move in elliptical motion, both up and down and back and forth.

Exercice 6

Today's class will be about Arnold Schoenberg and his twelve-tone or atonal technique. OK, so I suppose that if you have completed your assignment, you can tell me about atonality. Did you know, though, that Arnold Schoenberg was the first to contest the term « atonality » ? For him, « atonal » meant « without tone », and he argued furiously that his music was not lacking in tone at all. So, even though his music is sort of a statement against tonal hierarchies, he would have preferred the term « pan-tonal music » or « music without a tonal center ». In the long run, the official term remains « atonality ».

Did you also know that in 1907, the audience for Schoenberg's Chamber Symphony Number 1 was very small, and that the reception was worse than lukewarm ? As a matter of fact, at a concert of his and other musicians' atonal works in 1913, the police had to be called to the scene because the audience became rowdy. Music lovers were used to traditional tonality in music and this was too radical for them.

Have you yourself gone to the listening section of the library to do your listening assignment ? If you have taken the time to listen to Pierrot Lunaire, you will most likely know what I am referring to. The public's reaction to the twelve-tone system is usually black or white : either people hate the break from traditional tonality or they love the modern, revolutionary aspect of this music.

Now, what did you think of this piece of music sung in Sprechstimme ? This is the half speaking-half singing, uh, recitation, shall we call it ? Some may love it, but you have to admit that it is very, very different. Time has proven that a great majority of music-lovers will not throng to go hear Pierrot Lunaire in concert.

So, um... it is easy to conclude that Schoenberg's twelve-tone technique is controversial. Many people refuse to consider Schoenberg's works to be music at all. To top it off, in the field of music, there is a popular joke among musicians that goes like this : « The two great errors of the 20th century were atonality and Marxism. »

3. Sujets de rédaction supplémentaires

Independent Writing – Sujets supplémentaires

Voici quelques sujets extraits d'une annale de 2001, Information Bulletin for Computer-Based Testing :

1. You have enough money to purchase either a house or a business. Which would you choose to buy ? Give specific reasons to explain your choice.
2. What are some qualities of a good parent ? Use specific details and examples to explain your answer.
3. Some people believe that the Earth is being harmed (damaged) by human activity. Others feel that human activity makes the Earth a better place to live. What is your opinion ? Use specific reasons and examples to support your answer.
4. It is better for children to grow up in the countryside than in a big city. Do you agree or disagree ? Use specific reasons and examples to develop your essay.
5. Do you agree or disagree with the following statement ? Technology has made the world a better place to live. Use specific reasons and examples to support your opinion.
6. A foreign visitor has only one day to spend in your country. Where should this visitor go on that day ? Why ? Use specific reasons and details to support your choice.
7. Your school has received a gift of money. What do you think is the best way for your school to spend this money ? Use specific reasons and details to support your choice.
8. Do you agree or disagree with the following statement ? A zoo has no useful purpose. Use specific reasons and examples to explain your answer.
9. If you could make one important change in a school that you attended, what change would you make ? Use reasons and specific examples and details to support your choice.
10. Your school has enough money to purchase either computers for students or books for the library. Which should your school choose to buy – computers or books ? Use specific reasons and examples to support your recommendation.
11. You have decided to give several hours of your time each month to improve the community where you live. What is one thing you will do to improve your community ? Why ? Use specific reasons and details to explain your choice.

Conclusion

« Nous sommes courageux… Nous n'avons peur que d'une chose : c'est que le ciel nous tombe sur la tête… Nous aimons rigoler ! Nous aimons bien manger et bien boire… Nous sommes râleurs… Nous sommes indisciplinés et bagarreurs… mais nous aimons les copains ! Bref… nous sommes des Gaulois ! »

Une aventure d'Astérix le Gaulois, *La grande traversée*

Le TOEFL iBT, *Test of English as a Foreign Language, Internet Based Test*, examen spécifiquement américain, est le test d'évaluation du niveau en anglais le plus répandu dans le monde. Son nouveau format, dit « Next Generation », mesure la capacité d'intégrer un programme académique anglophone et de communiquer en anglais de manière opérationnelle. Que vous soyez étudiant dans une grande école en France ou que vous visiez à la voie universitaire aux Etat-Unis, cet examen représente un sésame qui vous ouvre des portes vers le diplôme de votre choix. C'est non seulement parce que cet examen est d'une importance capitale, mais aussi parce que le nouveau TOEFL iBT est beaucoup plus difficile que l'ancien, que ce livre a été conçu avec des renseignements et des conseils précis.

Le message de ce livre est une recommandation : **préparez-vous**, les Gaulois.

Educational Testing Service sait pertinemment que les Français sont les mauvais élèves de l'Europe en anglais. Il vous attend avec ses meilleurs pièges. Préparez-vous, car la préparation vaut son pesant de points supplémentaires.

- Entraînez-vous à la lecture de longs textes académiques. Apprenez à les parcourir pour aller plus vite, car le temps sera très court.
- Habituez votre oreille à l'accent américain et prenez l'habitude d'écouter de longs textes. Une bonne prise de notes sera primordiale le jour de l'examen.
- Soyez sûr d'avoir compris le format des questions dans la section Speaking à l'avance. Vous n'aurez pas le temps d'y réfléchir le jour J.
- Préparez votre trame de rédaction à l'avance et entraînez-vous à rédiger sur le clavier QWERTY. Le temps sera à peine suffisant.

Vous avez sûrement passé le Diagnostic Test du CD-ROM pour vous situer et pour mieux définir la tâche à accomplir et les progrès à réaliser. N'oubliez pas qu'il existe de véritables techniques à apprendre pour réussir le TOEFL iBT. Assimilez ces techniques, car elles seront essentielles le jour de l'examen.

Lucidité, préparation, volonté… voilà les outils nécessaires pour réussir le TOEFL iBT. Avec ces outils et le vent en poupe, tout étudiant gaulois sera prêt à entamer la grande traversée vers le Nouveau Monde.

Utilisation du CD-Rom

Configuration requise

PC avec processeur Pentium II 400, 128 Mo de RAM
Système d'exploitation Windows 98 ou supérieur.
Le logiciel Flash Player, nécessaire à la lecture du CD-Rom, s'installe automatiquement.
Macintosh avec processeur PowerPC, 64 Mo de RAM, Système d'exploitation MacOS 9 ou supérieur.
Le logiciel Flash Player, nécessaire à la lecture du CD-Rom, s'installe automatiquement

Pour utiliser ce CD-Rom dans un environnement Windows

Insérez le CD-Rom dans le lecteur.
La page d'accueil de notre CD-Rom s'ouvre automatiquement.
Vous pouvez démarrer votre examen ou vos exercices.

Pour utiliser ce CD-Rom (environnement MacOs)

Insérer le CD-Rom dans le lecteur.
Double-cliquer sur l'icone montée sur le bureau.
Vous pouvez démarrer votre examen ou vos exercices.

Contenu du CD-Rom

Ce CD-Rom contient le Diagnostic Tests, qui permet de s'entraîner dans les conditions du TOEFL iBT®, ainsi que des exercices.

L'éditeur ne pourra être tenu pour responsable des préjudices ou dommages de quelque nature que ce soit pouvant résulter de l'utilisation de ce CD-Rom.

Adressez vos réclamations éventuelles à :
multimedia@eyrolles.com

Composé par PCA
44400 Rezé

Achevé d'imprimer : EMD

N° d'éditeur : 3310
N° d'imprimeur : 16985
Dépôt légal : Mars 2007

Imprimé en France